Radhakrishnan

An Anthology

Radhakrishnan

An Anthology

Edited by
A. N. Marlow

PILGRIMS PUBLISHING
◆ Varanasi ◆

RADHAKRISHNAN: An Anthology
A. N. Marlow

Published by:
PILGRIMS PUBLISHING

An imprint of:
PILGRIMS BOOK HOUSE
(Distributors in India)
B 27/98 A-8, Nawabganj Road
Durga Kund, Varanasi-221010, India
Tel: 91-542- 2314060, 2312456
E-mail: pilgrims@satyam.net.in
Website: www.pilgrimsbooks.com

PILGRIMS BOOK HOUSE (New Delhi)
9 Netaji Subhash Marg, 2nd Floor
Near Neeru Hotel, Daryaganj, New Delhi 110002
Tel: 91-11-23285081 Fax: 91-11-23285722
E-mail: pilgrim@del2.vsnl.net.in

Distributed in Nepal by:
PILGRIMS BOOK HOUSE
P O Box 3872, Thamel, Kathmandu, Nepal
Tel: 977-1-4700942, Off: 977-1-4700919
Fax: 977-1-4700943
E-mail: pilgrims@wlink.com.np

Cover design by Asha Mishra

ISBN: 81-7769-302-6

Printed in India at Pilgrim Press Pvt. Ltd. Lalpur Varanasi

PREFACE TO THE NEW EDITION

Professor Sir Sarvepalli Radhakrishnan first came to public attention in 1918 when he wrote about the philosophy of Rabindranath Tagore. His career was devoted mainly to philosophy, but he also had the rare distinction of being a Professor at Oxford as well as being appointed Indian Ambassador to the Soviet Union in later years.

This anthology, edited by A. N. Marlow, has all the salient ingredients that make the works of Radhakrishnan so clear and enlightening to the student of philosophy. He examines many subjects, from pure Hindu thought to Buddhist failings and Christian shortcomings. He delves into the subject of Samkara, the revivalist pioneer of Hindu philosophy. Radhakrishnan continually questions the very fabric of all the ideals, particularly in relationship to the revival set down by Samkara. He accuses Samkara, who reintroduced the basic ancient format of Hindu philosophy, of being virtually an ascetic, bordering on an atheist. The author of these edited excerpts, Marlow uses quotes from Mahatma Gandhi where his words add to the dimension of the main theme.

"...we find Samkara arguing that the life of the spirit is repressed and hampered by union with the material body."

Radhakrishnan became during his lifetime an icon for intellectuals, those in constant search for the true light, the true direction and meaning of life. But all this is of course merely expressions of differing viewpoints. All the ideas that emanate from the basic ideals of Hindu philosophy are focused on the individual discovering the ultimate purpose of the spirit or soul. One can analyse these wise words and make one's own judgement

Radhakrishnan's work will inspire, give cause for deep mental consideration, act as a revelation and generally provoke the reader to examine the ultimate truths of life.

Bob Gibbons
Siân Pritchard-Jones
Kathmandu 2004

CONTENTS

PREFACE

FOR thirty years the influence of Sir Sarvépalli Radhakrishnan has been steadily growing. To-day his writings on philosophy and religion reach a world-wide audience, and tributes are being paid to him by the publication of a series of philosophical studies in honour of his sixtieth birthday and by the appearance of a volume devoted to him in the American *Library of Living Philosophers*. Yet in view of the universal and fundamental importance of his words on the religion of spirit, some more popular presentation of his work is desirable in order that many more may acquaint themselves with its charm and scope, and be led to read further.

Professor Radhakrishnan, like St. Bernard of Clairvaux, adds to a scholar's achievement a career of action. After being professor of philosophy at Madras, Mysore and Calcutta and vice-chancellor at Waltair he was appointed in 1936 to the newly-created Spalding Professorship in Eastern Religions and Ethics at Oxford, an appointment which he still holds. Previously his Upton and Hibbert Lectures in 1926 and 1929 and his Haskell Lectures in Chicago in 1926 had attracted wide attention. From 1931 to 1939 he was a member of the League of Nations committee on intellectual co-operation and in 1948 he became chairman of the Universities Commission of the Government of India. In 1949 he was appointed chairman of the Executive Board of Unesco and in the same year became Ambassador for India to the Soviet Union. This bald catalogue mentions no more than a tithe of the posts he has honourably filled. Thus if he cannot claim to be a philosopher king in the fully Platonic sense of the word he comes as near to the fulfilment of that ideal as is possible in these days.

His earliest book was on the philosophy of Rabindranath Tagore and was published in 1918. Penetrating and charming though this book is I have not laid it under contribution for this anthology because I understand that the author does not regard it as fully representative of his mature work and has not re-issued it. Apart from this I have included selections from all his books and from many of his articles in the *Hibbert Journal* to which he has regularly contributed. A bibliography is printed for the behoof of readers, as A. E. Housman would have said.

I have given special prominence to the theme which recurs throughout these writings, the need for a universal religion of spirit that shall begin within a man's own soul and work outwardly through all his relations with men and with nature. This religion of spirit has been advocated before by Hindus from the time of Ram Mohan Ray, but nearly always the religion has been either Hinduism pure and simple or a thinly veiled and unsatisfactory eclecticism. Professor Radhakrishnan's starting-point is the Upaniṣads, as he shows in his early work *The Reign of Religion in Contemporary Philosophy*, but he has a unique viewpoint in that he is steeped in Western as well as in Eastern philosophy and has lived in the West as a scholar and man of affairs: thus his views and convictions have a centrality and an authority denied to most others. Of the charm and eloquence of his style I will leave the anthology to speak. The most forceful statement of his ideals and of his judgment of the contemporary situation is in his *Hibbert Lectures* reprinted as *An Idealist View of Life*, and again in his *Religion and Society*, based on lectures delivered in Indian Universities in 1942. His *Eastern Religions and Western Thought*, published in 1939, is more concerned, as its title suggests, with the religious and philosophical impact of Hinduism on the West through the centuries.

Professor Radhakrishnan speaks, of course, with particular authority on the subject of Hindu thought, and his two volumes published in 1923 and 1926 on Indian philosophy are in my opinion his greatest work. I have included a number of extracts from them, particularly from the first volume on the Vedas, the Upaniṣads and Buddhism because to my mind nowhere in English is there an account of the various Indian systems that combines authoritativeness and charm in an equal degree. It is less easy to select from the second volume which deals with the six systems, as there is a multiplicity of detail which never gets out of control but which cannot very well be read in selections.

It is not in fact easy to compile an anthology of these works, as Professor Radhakrishnan writes with a sustained loftiness of aim which makes one desire to go on quoting indefinitely. In expounding a saying of Buddha or Saṁkara—and Hindus have always excelled as commentators—he draws out the full spiritual meaning, often adding comment from his own deep store, until passage after passage has a sustained glow. Yet he can be crisply epigrammatic, and I have added a tentative and inadequate selection of his *obiter dicta*, which will at any rate balance the length of some of the passages from his philosophical works.

To Hindu thinking all philosophy must begin with the necessary discipline of body, a complete relaxation and withdrawal from all outward preoccupation; so I have taken this *ascesis* as my starting point. After this the order of subjects would perhaps be generally agreed on, but in its details I have no doubt that others would have proceeded differently, and I must ask their pardon. I am not a professional philosopher and can only claim a deep interest in Professor Radhakrishnan's writings and the friendship of their author as qualifications. In any case it is now time to let him speak for himself.

My acknowledgments are due to the Oxford University Press for permission to print three extracts from the introduction to Professor Radhakrishnan's translation of *The Dhammapada*, published in 1950.

NORMAN MARLOW

The University,
Manchester

AIM OF PHILOSOPHY

Our life is a step on a road, the direction and goal of which are lost in the infinite. On this road, death is never an end or an obstacle but at most the beginning of new steps. The development of the soul is a continuous process, though it is broken into stages by the recurring baptism of death.

Philosophy carries us to the gates of the promised land, but cannot let us in; for that, insight or realisation is necessary. We are like children stranded in the darkness of saṁsāra, with no idea of our true nature, and inclined to imagine fears and to cling to hopes in the gloom that surrounds us. Hence arises the need for light, which will free us from the dominion of passions and show us the real which we unwittingly are, and the unreal in which we ignorantly live.

INDIAN PHILOSOPHY, II, p. 27

The survey of Indian thought, as of all thought, impresses one with the mystery and the immensity of existence as well as the beauty and the persistence of the human effort to understand it. The long procession of thinkers struggled hard to add some small piece to the temple of human wisdom, some fresh fragment to the ever incomplete sum of human knowledge. But human speculation falls short of the ideal, which it can neither abandon nor attain. We are far more conscious of the depth of the surrounding darkness than of the power to dispel it possessed by the flickering torches that we have the privilege to carry as the inheritors of a great past. After all the attempts of philosophers, we stand to-day in relation to the ultimate problems very near where we stood far away in the ages—where perhaps we shall ever stand as long as we are human, bound Prometheus-like to the rock of mystery by the chains of our finite mind. The pursuit of philosophy is not, however, a vain endeavour. It helps us to feel the grip and the clanging of the chains. It sharpens the consciousness of human imperfection, and thus deepens the sense of perfection in us, which reveals the imperfection of our passing lives. That the world is not so transparent to our intellects as we could wish is not to be wondered at, for the philosopher is only the lover of wisdom and not its possessor. It is not the end of the voyage that matters, but the voyage itself. To travel is a better thing than to arrive.

At the end of our course, we may ask whether the known facts of history support a belief in progress. Is the march of human thought a forward movement, or is it one of retrogression? The sequence is not capricious and unmeaning. India believes in progress, for, as we have already said, the cycles are bound together by an organic tie. The inner thread of continuity is never cut. Even the revolutions that threaten to engulf the past help to restore it. Backward eddies serve rather to strengthen than retard the current. Epochs of decadence, like the recent past of this country, are in truth periods of transition from an old life to a new. The two currents of progress and decline are intermingled. At one stage the forces of progress press forward with a persistent sweep, at another the line sways to and fro, and sometimes the forces of retrogression seem to overwhelm those of progress, but on the whole the record is one of advance. It would be idle to deny that much has perished in the process. But few things are more futile than to rail against the course which the historical past has taken or weep over it. In any case, some other kind of development would have been worse. The more important thing is the future. We are able to see farther than our predecessors, since we can climb on their shoulders. Instead of resting content with the foundations nobly laid in the past, we must build a greater edifice in harmony with ancient endeavour as well as the modern outlook.

INDIAN PHILOSOPHY, II, pp. 767–8

From this it is plain that philosophy has an essential function in the life of spirit, if it only rests on experience and develops on its basis. That is what all serious philosophy has been. As satisfying an inherent need of reason, philosophy has its place in the life of mind.

REIGN OF RELIGION IN CONTEMPORARY PHILOSOPHY, p. 300

PRELIMINARY DISCIPLINE

THE seeker after truth must satisfy certain essential conditions before he sets out on his quest. Śaṁkara, in his commentary on the first Sūtra of the Vedānta Sūtras, makes out that four conditions are essential for any student of philosophy. The first condition is a knowledge of the distinction between the eternal and the non-eternal. This does not mean full knowledge, which can come only at the end, but only a metaphysical bent which does not accept all it sees to be absolutely real, a questioning tendency in the inquirer. He must have the inquiring spirit to probe all things, a burning imagination which could extract a truth from a mass of apparently disconnected data, and a habit of meditation which will not allow his mind to dissipate itself. The second condition is the subjugation of the desire for the fruits of action either in the present life or a future one. It demands the renunciation of all petty desire, personal motive and practical interest. Speculation or inquiry to the reflective mind is its own end. The right employment of intellect is understanding things, good as well as bad. The philosopher is a naturalist who should follow the movement of things without exaggerating the good or belittling the evil on behalf of some prejudice of his. He must stand outside of life and look on it. So it is said that he must have no love of the present or the future. Only then can he stake his all on clear thinking and honest judgment and develop an impersonal cosmic outlook with devotedness to fact. To get this temper he must suffer a change of heart, which is insisted on in the third condition, where the student is enjoined to acquire tranquillity, self-restraint, renunciation, patience, peace of mind and faith. Only a trained mind which utterly controls the body can inquire and meditate endlessly so long as life remains, never for a moment losing sight of the object, never for a moment letting it be obscured by any terrestrial temptation. The seeker after truth must have the necessary courage to lose all for his highest end. So is he required to undergo hard discipline, spurn pleasure, suffer sorrow and contempt. A spiritual discipline which includes pitiless self-examination will enable the seeker to reach his end of freedom. The desire for mokṣa or release is the fourth condition. The metaphysically minded man who has given up all desires and trained his mind has only one devouring desire—to achieve the end or reach the eternal. The people of India have such an immense respect for these philosophers who glory in the might of knowledge and the power of intellect, that they worship them. The prophetic souls who with a noble passion for truth strive hard to understand the mystery of the world and give utterance to it, spending laborious days and sleepless nights, are philosophers in a vital sense of the term. They comprehend experience on behalf of mankind, and so the latter are eternally grateful to them.

INDIAN PHILOSOPHY, I, pp. 45–6

The extent to which we know reality depends on the state of our mind, whether it can respond to the full wealth of reality or not. Colours are not revealed to the blind nor music to the deaf, nor philosophic truth to the feeble-minded. The process of knowing is not so much a creation as a discovery, not so much a production as a revelation. It follows that the revelation will be imperfect or distorted, if there is any taint or imperfection clinging to the instrument. The selfish desires and passions get between the instrument of mind and the reality to be revealed. When the personality of the subject affects the nature of the instrument, the reflection becomes blurred. The ignorance of the observer clouds the object with his fancies. His prevailing prejudices are cast over the truth of things. Error is just the intrusion into the reality of the defects of the instrument. An impartial and impersonal attitude is necessary for the discovery of truth, and all that is merely personal impedes this process. We must be saved from the malformation and the miscarriage of our minds. The clamant energies of the mind must be bent to become the passive channels for the transmission of truth. The Yoga method gives directions how to refine the mind and improve the mirror, keeping it clean by keeping out what is peculiar to the individual. It is only through this discipline that we can rise to that height of strenuous impersonality from which the gifted souls of the world see distant visions. This method is in consonance with the Upaniṣad theory of the self. Our ordinary consciousness turns its back on the eternal world and is lost in the perishing unreal world cast by the mind out of sense impressions. When we rise above the empirical self we get not a negation but an intensification of self. When the self is bound down to its empirical accidents, its activities are not fully exercised. When the limitations of empirical existence are transcended, universal life is intensified, and we have an enrichment of self or enhancement of personality. Then it draws all experience into it. In the lower stages, when the self is identified with any definite centre generated by the accidents of time and space, the world of experience is not made its own. The adherence to a narrow circle of experience must be overcome before we can gather into ourselves the world of experience, whose centre as well as circumference is God and man. Then we rise to a condition in which, in the words of the Upaniṣads, 'there is no difference between what is within and what is without.' The Yoga method insists that the false outward outlook must be checked before the true inward ideal is given a chance of life and expression. We must cease to live in the world of shadows before we can lay hold of the eternal life.

The Yoga system requires us to go through a course of mental and spiritual discipline. The Upaniṣads also emphasise the practice of austere virtues before the end can be reached. In the Prasna Upaniṣad Pippalāda sends away six inquirers after God for another year of discipline with the command, 'Go ye and spend another year in leading the life of celibacy (brahmacarya), in practising asceticism, in cherishing reverential faith (śraddhā).' The life of celibacy, where the student will have no family attachment to perturb his mind, would enable him to give whole-hearted attention to his work. The penances will give him mental quiet and remove the restlessness of mind which is such a great obstacle to knowledge. Śraddhā or faith is necessary for all work. The essence of Yoga philosophy, as of all mystic teaching, is the insistence on the possibility of coming into direct contact with the divine consciousness by raising the human to a plane above its normal level.

We must control the mind which binds us to outer things and makes slaves of us, to realise freedom. Being the victims of outer objects and circumstances, we do not reach satisfaction. 'As rain-water that has fallen on a mountain ridge runs down on all sides, thus does he who sees a difference between qualities run after them on all sides. As pure water poured into pure water remains the same, thus, O Gautama, is the self of a thinker who knows.' The mind of a man who does not know his own self goes hither and thither like the water pouring down the crags in every direction. But when his mind is purified, he becomes one with the great ocean of life which dwells behind all mortal forms. The outward mind, if allowed free scope, gets dispersed in the desert sands. The seeker must draw it inward, hold it still to obtain the treasure within. We have to force utterance into feeling, feeling into thought, and thought into universal consciousness; only then do we become conscious of the deep peace of the eternal.

INDIAN PHILOSOPHY, I, pp. 260–3

The ālaya is sometimes the actual self, developing and ever-growing. It receives impressions and develops the germs deposited in it by karma, or experience, and is continually active. It is not merely the superficial self, but the great storehouse of consciousness which the yogins find out by meditation. Through meditation and other practices of self-examination, we realise that our waking or superficial consciousness is a fragment of a wider whole. Every individual has in him this vast whole of consciousness, the great tank of the contents of which the conscious self is not fully aware.

INDIAN PHILOSOPHY, I, p. 629

The reality of the self is to be found not by means of an objective use of the mind, but by a suppression of its activities and penetration beneath the mental strata with which our ordinary life and activity conceal our diviner nature. Though the seed of spirit is present in each one of us, it is not realised by our consciousness, which is too busily engaged with other things. We must undergo a severe discipline before we can achieve the redirection of our consciousness. The Yoga philosophy urges that the necessary inhibition of mental states is brought about by practice and conquest of desire. While the latter is the result of a life of virtue, the former refers to the effort towards steadiness of thought, which is gained by purificatory action, continence, knowledge and faith. Vairāgya or passionlessness, is the consciousness of mastery possessed by one who has rid himself of thirst for either seen or revealed objects. Such a one is supremely indifferent to the pleasures of heaven or of earth. In the highest form of vairagya, where the discernment of the self arises, there is no danger of any subjection to the desire for objects or their qualities. This leads to ultimate freedom, while the lower form of vairāgya, which has a trace of rajas (and so pravṛtti) in it, results in the condition of absorption in prakṛti (prakṛtilaya).

INDIAN PHILOSOPHY, II, pp. 351–2

We should practise ahiṁsā, or non-violence, truthfulness, honesty, continence and non-acceptance of gifts, i.e. we should abstain from the inflicting of injury, from falsehood, theft, incontinence and avarice. The chief of them all is ahiṁsā, or non-violence, and all other virtues are said to be rooted in it. Ahiṁsā is interpreted broadly as abstinence from malice towards all living creatures in every way and at all times. It is not merely non-violence but non-hatred (vairatyagah). The cultivation of friendliness, sympathy, cheerfulness and imperturbability with regard to things, pleasant and painful, good and bad, produces serenity of mind (cittaprasādanam). We must be free from jealousy and not be callous to the suffering of others. While hating sin, we must be gentle to the sinner. No exceptions are allowed to these principles, which are absolute in their character. 'Kill not' is a categorical imperative, and we cannot compromise its absoluteness by holding that we can kill the enemies of our country, or the deserters from the army, or the renegades of religion, or the blasphemers of the Brahmins. Not even self-defence can justify murder. The yamas are of universal validity regardless of differences of caste and country, age and condition. They are to be acquired by all, though all may not be chosen for the higher life of contemplation.

INDIAN PHILOSOPHY, II, pp. 353–4

The body can be made the basis of either animal incontinence or divine strength. We are asked to be careful about our food. We should not eat and drink things which set our nerves on edge, driving them into fever or stupor. The lower satisfactions of life generally strangle the true joy of spirit. If intellectual life and moral activity are the true ends of man, then the bodily needs should be subordinated to them. The later stages of the Yoga demand great powers of physical endurance, and cases are not wanting where the strenuous spiritual life strains the earthen vessel to the breaking-point, and so the body has to be first brought under control. Haṭha Yoga aims at perfecting the bodily instrument, freeing it from its liability to fatigue and arresting its tendency to decay and age.

The Yoga asks us to control the body and not kill it. Abstinence from sensual indulgences is not the same as the crucifixion of the body, but the two have sometimes been confused in Hindu India as well as Christian Europe. The Yoga says that the perfection of the body consists in beauty, grace, strength and adamantine hardness.

INDIAN PHILOSOPHY, II, pp. 355–6

THE NATURE OF REALITY

If the dream-states do not fit into the context of the general experience of our fellow men or of our own normal experience, it must be understood that it is not because they fall short of absolute reality, but because they do not conform to our conventional standards. They substitute a separate class of experiences, and, within their order, they are coherent. The water in the dream can quench the thirst in the dream, and to say that it does not quench the real thirst is irrelevant. To say so is to assume that waking experience is real in itself and is the only real. The two, waking- and dream-states, are equally real within their own orders or equally unreal in an absolute sense. Gaudapāda recognises that the objects of waking experience are common to us all, while those of dreams are the private property of the dreamer. Yet he says: 'As in dream, so in waking, the objects seen are unreal.' His contention is that whatever is presented as an object is unreal. The argument that all objects are unreal and only the subject that is the constant witness self is real, is suggested in some Upaniṣads and developed with negative results in Buddhistic thought. It is now employed by Gaudapāda to prove that life is a waking dream. We accept the waking world as objective, not because we experience other people's mental states, but because we accept their testimony. The relations of space, time and cause, which govern the objects of the waking world, need not be considered to be ultimate. According to Gaudapāda, 'By the nature of a thing is understood that which is complete in itself, that which is its very condition, that which is inborn, that which is not accidental, or that which does not cease to be itself.' When we apply such a test, we find that both the souls and the world are nothing by themselves and are Ātman only.

INDIAN PHILOSOPHY, II, pp. 454–5

Our senses may deceive us and our memory may be an illusion. The past and the future may be abstractions. The forms of the world may be pure fancy, and all our life may be a tragic illusion. Nothing prevents us from regarding the waking tracts of experience as analogous to dream-worlds, where also we visit places, handle shadows and do battle with ghosts, and remember, too, all our adventures in the fairyland. If dreams are facts, facts may well be dreams. Though all objects of knowledge may be matters of belief and so open to doubt, there seems to be still something in experience transcending it.

INDIAN PHILOSOPHY, II, p. 475

It is one thing to say that the secret of existence, how the unchangeable reality expresses itself in the changing universe without forfeiting its nature, is a mystery, and another to dismiss the whole changing universe as a mere mirage. If we have to play the game of life, we cannot do so with the conviction that the play is a show and all the prizes in it mere blanks. No philosophy can consistently hold such a view and be at rest with itself. The greatest condemnation of such a theory is that we are obliged to occupy ourselves with objects, the existence and value of which we are continually denying in theory. The fact of the world may be mysterious and inexplicable. It only shows that there is something else which includes and transcends the world; but it does not imply that the world is a dream.

INDIAN PHILOSOPHY, II, p. 463

Mere presence to an individual consciousness is not the esse of a thing. Even when we perceive pain, it is not a mere mental affection. It is as objective and existent as any object of consciousness. We perceive things as they are, and they are what they appear to be. Even metaphysically, as we shall see, Śaṁkara is obliged to posit an object, for consciousness is mere knowing or awareness. It has no content, no states. It is a pure, featureless transparency. The colour, the richness, the movement and the tumult are all on the object side. We distinguish between sensing, perceiving, remembering, imagining, reflecting, judging, reasoning, believing, because the objects of consciousness are different. Pure consciousness neither gives nor receives. Even in erroneous perception there is some object. That is why for Śaṁkara, as for Bradley, there are no absolute truths, as there are no mere errors. Only, while true ideas answer to our needs and fit into our conception of reality as a systematic whole, erroneous ideas refuse to do so. The world, seen, felt, tasted and touched, is as real as the being of the man who sees, feels, tastes and touches. The mind with its categories, on the one side, and the world which it construes through them on the other, hang together.

INDIAN PHILOSOPHY, II, pp. 497–8

Objects have no existence for themselves, and if they are not the contents of my or your consciousness, they are the contents of the divine consciousness. To the divine consciousness world-systems are present, full of contents and selves that are aware of their contents. The continuous divine percipient accounts for the permanent world-order. He is superior to the finite selves and objects in his infinity of content and complete presence to himself. He is the universal spirit who creates and is aware of the contents of the universe. As we deal with our private contents, so does God deal with the world-systems. This larger world and the divine consciousness for which it is are both contracted into subordinate centres which are only partially free. All contents are sustained by the divine consciousness, and were the latter known intensely enough it would be a veritable sea of consciousness. When the individual awakes to life, breaks down the contracting upādhis which limit his vision, he will realise that the whole world is filled with Ātman inside and out, even as the water of the sea is filled with salt. Strictly speaking, all contents of the universe are spiritual in their character.

INDIAN PHILOSOPHY, II, pp. 498–9

The more we reflect on the matter the more impossible it seems to assert that the world known to us under the conditions of empirical knowledge is the real in itself. The man with five senses knows more than the blind man. May not the real exceed the empirical conception of it, even as the world known to sight exceeds that known to touch? May not a state like that of brahmānubhava, or what Tennyson has called a "last and largest sense," enlarge our own knowledge of reality, as the gift of sight would enlarge that of a race of blind men? This view does not involve any scepticism with regard to the world of science and common sense. So long as we do not reach a higher plane attainable only by higher intelligences, our conclusions are quite valid, except that they remain on the same plane as their premises.

INDIAN PHILOSOPHY, II, p. 504

Our intellect is so made that it demands order and regularity in things. It resents accident and disorder. The world of objects is rational through and through, and answers to the demand of reason for law and order in all things. This is the faith of common sense and science. Śaṁkara does not sever thought from things. The principles of our mind, expressing themselves through the categories of space, time and cause, are at once the forms of combination which make up the nature of the thinking subject and also the forms that are to be met with in the realm of objective fact. The categories of intelligence apply to the things presented to it. This space-time-cause world, with all its contents, exists for the knowing subject. The two depend on each other, the empirical self and the world. This fact of the response of nature to the demand of reason proves the reality of a universal mind, which on the one hand ensouls nature and on the other is the cause of the reason in us, participating in and co-operating with the universal mind. The reality of an ordered world exists only for mind and in terms of mind. The world of an animal presupposes the mind of an animal; that of man, the mind of man. The whole world reality in its fullness and complexity postulates a universal and perfect mind, Īsvara, who sustains those parts of the universe which are unperceived by us.

INDIAN PHILOSOPHY, II, pp. 508–9

The subtleties of the schools are all silenced before the protest of the soul that it has seen reality. How can one contest the fact of another possessing the knowledge of Brahman, though still in the body, vouched as it is by his heart's conviction? All faith and devotion, all study and meditation, are intended to train us for this experience. Intuition of self, however, comes only to a mind prepared for it. It does not come out of the blue. It is the noblest blossoming of man's reason. It is not a mere fancy which refuses to make an appeal to man's intelligence. What is true is true for every intelligence that can apprehend it.

There is no such thing as a private truth, any more than a private sun or a private science. Truth has an intrinsic and universal character, which depends on no individual, not even on God. The process of apprehending reality may be private or singular, but not the object apprehended. The real cannot be real now and then, here and there, but always and everywhere.

INDIAN PHILOSOPHY, II, p. 512

If we depend on thought, we have to doubt the world, doubt our being, doubt the future, and end our life in doubt. But since we must either react on our environment or be destroyed by it, the force of the life within drives us irresistibly to faith. There are spiritual impulses which refuse to be set aside at the bidding of logic. No one can live on negation.

INDIAN PHILOSOPHY, II, p. 516

From the beginning to the end of things it is always a question of light invading the realm of darkness. We may push it farther and farther. It only recedes, but never disappears. The relation of being to non-being in the finite world is not one of exclusion but one of polar opposition. The ideas are at once antithetic and correlative. Neither of them attains actuality except through its contrast with the other. However much the one may penetrate the other or be penetrated by it, the distinction and contrast are always there, so that everything in the world is unstable and doomed to be fugitive. Even the highest principle in the world process, the personal God, has in him the shadow of non-being. Brahman alone is pure being, possessing whatever there is of reality in all things, without their limitations or elements of non-being. Whatever is different from it is unreal.

INDIAN PHILOSOPHY, II, p. 564

The enfranchisement of man from all his self-wrought bondages, the glory which is utterly beyond all grasp of thought, the peace that is the very purpose of all our striving, lies nearer to us than our nearest consciousness. Saṁkara shows us not a heaven which is apart from, a different order of experience from, earth, but the heaven which is all the time here, could we but see it. It is not something in an imagined future, a continuance of existence in a world to come after the present life is ended, but a state of identification with the real here and now.

INDIAN PHILOSOPHY, II, p. 636

The activities of the self are assigned to the three states of waking, dreaming and dreamless sleep. In dream-states an actual concrete world is presented to us. We do not call that world real, since on waking we find that the dream-world does not fit in with the waking world; yet relatively to the dream-state the dream-world is real. It is discrepancy from our conventional standards of waking life, and not any absolute knowledge of truth as subsisting by itself, that tells us that dream-states are less real than the waking ones. Even waking reality is a relative one. It has no permanent existence, being only a correlate of the waking state. It disappears in dream and sleep. The waking consciousness and the world disclosed to it are related to each other, depend on each other as the dream-consciousness and the dream-world are. They are not absolutely real, for in the words of Saṁkara, while the 'dream-world is daily sublated, the waking world is sublated under exceptional circumstances.' In dreamless sleep we have a cessation of the empirical consciousness. The Indian thinkers are of opinion that we have in this condition an objectless consciousness. At any rate this is clear, that dreamless sleep is not a complete non-being or negation for such a hypothesis conflicts with the later recollection of the happy repose of sleep. We cannot help conceding that the self continues to exist, though it is bereft of all experience. There is no object felt and there can be none so long as the sleep is sound. The pure self seems to be unaffected by the flotsam and jetsam of ideas which rise and vanish with particular moods. 'What varies not, nor changes in the midst of things that vary and change is different from them.' The self which persists unchanged and is one throughout all the changes is different from them all. The conditions change, not the self. 'In all the endless months, years and small and great cycles, past and to come, this self-luminous consciousness alone neither rises nor ever sets.' An unconditioned reality where time and space along with all their objects vanish is felt to be real. It is the self which is the unaffected spectator of the whole drama of ideas related to the changing moods of waking, dreaming and sleeping. We are convinced that there is something in us beyond joy and misery, virtue and vice, good and bad. The self 'never dies, is never born—unborn, eternal, everlasting, this ancient one can never be destroyed with the destruction of the body. If the slayer thinks he can slay, or if the slain thinks he is slain, they both do not know the truth, for the self neither slays nor is slain.'

INDIAN PHILOSOPHY, I, pp. 32–3

Cf. Emerson's Brahma:

If the red slayer thinks he slays,
Or if the slain thinks he is slain,
They know not well the subtle ways
I keep and pass and turn again.

TRUE KNOWLEDGE

As becoming is a lapse from being, so is avidyā or ignorance a fall from vidyā or knowledge. To know the truth, to apprehend reality, we have to get rid of avidyā and its intellectual moulds, which all crack the moment we try to force reality into them. This is no excuse for indolence of thought. Philosophy as logic on this view persuades us to give up the employment of the intellectual concepts which are relative to our practical needs and the world of becoming. Philosophy tells us that, so long as we are bound by intellect and are lost in the world of many, we shall seek in vain to get back to the simplicity of the one. If we ask the reason why there is avidyā, or māyā, bringing about a fall from vidyā or from being, the question cannot be answered. Philosophy as logic has here the negative function of exposing the inadequacy of all intellectual categories, pointing out how the objects of the world are relative to the mind that thinks them and possess no independent existence. It cannot tell us anything definite about either the immutable said to exist apart from what is happening in the world, or about māyā, credited with the production of the world. It cannot help us directly to the attainment of reality. It, on the other hand, tells us that to measure reality we have to distort it. It may perhaps serve the interests of truth when once it is independently ascertained. We can think it out, defend it logically and help its propagation. The supporters of pure monism recognise a higher power than abstract intellect which enables us to feel the push of reality. We have to sink ourselves in the universal consciousness and make ourselves co-extensive with all that is. We do not then so much think reality as live it, do not so much know it as become it. Such an extreme monism, with its distinctions of logic and intuition, reality and the world of existence, we meet with in some Upaniṣads, Nāgārjuna and Śaṁkara in his ultra-philosophical moods, Śrī Harṣa and the Advaita Vedāntins, and echoes of it are heard in Parmenides and Plato, Spinoza and Plotinus, Bradley and Bergson, not to speak of the mystics, in the West.

INDIAN PHILOSOPHY, I, pp. 36–7

Knowledge is not something to be packed away in some corner of our brain, but what enters into our being, colours our emotion, haunts our soul, and is as close to us as life itself. It is the over-mastering power which through the intellect moulds the whole personality, trains the emotions and disciplines the will.

INDIAN PHILOSOPHY, I, p. 431

THE ABSOLUTE

ULTIMATELY, life mechanism, consciousness and intellect are parts of this comprehensive whole. They are all abstracts from it, and the Absolute is the only *res completa*. It is the only individual. We cannot attribute a substantial existence to the individuals of sense. If we do so we remain, to use Spinoza's language, at the level of imagination without rising to the level of reason. The Absolute, therefore, is the whole, the only individual, and the sum of all perfection. The differences are reconciled in it, and not obliterated. The dead mechanism of stones, the unconscious life of plants, the conscious life of animals, and the self-conscious life of men are all part of the Absolute and its expression at different stages. The same Absolute reveals itself in all these, but differently in each. The ultimate reality sleeps in the stone, breathes in the plants, feels in the animals and awakes to self-consciousness in man. We see the unity that links being to being, the unity of spirit which slowly passes from inert matter to living plants and so on, upwards through great travail gathering itself into its own substance until we reach God. It progressively manifests itself in and through these particulars. The Absolute thus is an organised whole, with interrelated parts in it. It embraces time, its events and processes. The finite universe is rooted in the Absolute. Life, mechanism, etc., are all members together of one whole. The Absolute is not an abstract unit, but a concrete whole binding together the differences which are subordinate to it. The whole has existence through the parts, and the parts are intelligible only through the whole. The values we find and enjoy while on the way to it are preserved and receive their full supplementation in it. They are not annihilated.

On this view there cannot be any 'creation.' The question as to why the Absolute limited itself, why God became man, why the perfect became imperfect, is irrelevant. For there is no such thing as infinite which first was an infinite and then transformed itself into the finite. The infinite is the finite. The Absolute is the self and its other. Gaudapāda in his Kārikas on the Māṇḍūkya Upaniṣad mentions the different theories of the creation of the universe. The universe may be the creation of an extra-cosmic God, or an illusion, or the product of evolution. He dismisses these theories as incorrect, and declares that it is of the nature of God to express himself. It is the essence of spirit to manifest itself. The word Brahman which stands for the Absolute in the Vedānta philosophy is derived from the root "brih"—to grow. It is the nature of the Absolute to grow into the world. The world is the affirmation of the Absolute. The universe is the energising of God. God realises himself in the world. We do not have the infinite and the finite, God and the world, but only the infinite as and in the finite, God as and in the world. The Supreme, the Eternal, is the unity of all things finite and infinite.

REIGN OF RELIGION IN CONTEMPORARY PHILOSOPHY, pp. 442–4

To say that Brahman is reality is to say that it is different from the phenomenal, the spatial, the temporal and the sensible. Brahman is what is assumed as foundational, though it is in no sense substance. It is not in any point of space, though it may be said to be everywhere, since all things imply and depend on it. Since it is not a thing, it cannot have spatial relations to anything else, and is therefore nowhere. It is not a cause, for that would be to introduce time relations. Its nature is inexpressible, for when we say anything of it we make it into a particular thing. We may speak about it, though we cannot describe it adequately or have any logical knowledge of it. If the finite man can comprehend Brahman, then either our understanding must be infinite or Brahman finite. 'Every word employed to denote a thing denotes that thing as associated with a certain genus, or act, or quality, or mode of relation.' Brahman has no genus, possesses no qualities, does not act, and is related to nothing else. It is devoid of anything of a like kind or of a different kind, and has no internal variety. A tree, for example, has the internal variety of leaves, flowers and fruits, has the relation of likeness to other trees and of unlikeness to objects of a different kind like stones. Brahman has nothing similar to it, nothing different from it, and no internal differentiation, since all these are empirical distinctions. As it is opposed to all empirical existence, it is given to us as the negative of everything that is positively known. Śaṁkara declines to characterise it even as one, but calls it non-dual, advaitam. It is the 'wholly other,' but not non-being. Though the words used are negative, what is meant is intensely positive. A negation is only an affirmation of absence. It is non-being, since it is not the being which we attribute to the world of experience. It does not follow that it is pure nothing, since the negative has its meaning only in relation to the positive. The Upaniṣads, as well as Śaṁkara, deny of Brahman both being and non-being of the type with which we are familiar in the world of experience. We can at best say what Brahman is not, and not what it is. It transcends the opposition of permanence and change, whole and part, relative and absolute, finite and infinite, which are all based on the oppositions of experience. The finite is always passing beyond itself, but there is nothing which the infinite can pass into. If it did so, it would no longer be the infinite. If we call it infinite, it is not to be equated with a mere negation of the finite. We cannot understand the nature of Brahman until we let go the formal and the finite. Since personality cannot be realised except under the limiting condition of a non-ego, the absolute is not a person. If we use the term personality in a different sense, in which it does not demand any dependence on another, then it is an illegitimate use. When the Absolute is said to be nirguṇa, this only means that it is trans-empirical, since guṇas are products of prakṛti and the Absolute is superior to it. The guṇas qualify the objective as such, and God is not an object. The objects come and go, but the real persists as the permanent in the midst of all changes. So it transcends the guṇas or phenomenal being. The Absolute is not on that account to be regarded as a mere blank. So the Upaniṣad says 'nirguṇo guṇi.' Brahman is of the nature of ultimate consciousness and yet knows nothing, since empirical cognition is a modification of the internal organ. Knowledge, again, is its essence and not its property. It is not eternal in the sense of persisting changelessly through time like the motionless being of Parmenides, the 'mindless, unmoving fixture,' which Plato derides in the Sophist, but in the sense of absolute timelessness and incorruptibility. It is eternal because its completeness and perfection are unrelated to time. The sequence which binds things and events in the time-order has no meaning for it. It is eternal perdurance, to which all time-relations are irrelevant.

INDIAN PHILOSOPHY, II, pp. 534–7

A 'Personal God' has meaning only for the practical religious consciousness and not for the highest insight. To the finite individual blinded by the veils, the Absolute seems to be determinate and exclusive of himself. Bondage and redemption possess a meaning for the finite individual, whose consciousness is fettered and repressed by his lower nature. If a personal God exclusive of the individual were the highest, then mystic experiences would become unintelligible, and we should have to remain content with a finite God. God is no God if he is not the All; if he be the All, then religious experience is not the highest. If God's nature is perfect, it cannot be so, so long as man's imperfect nature stands over against it; if it is not perfect, then it is not the nature of God. There is thus a fundamental contradiction in religious experience, clearly indicating that it belongs to the province of avidyā.

INDIAN PHILOSOPHY, II, pp. 650–1

The Absolute transcends not merely its finite but also its infinite expressions taken singly or in a finite number. In its range, of expression or degree of expressiveness, the Absolute transcends all finite limits. The question of immanence and transcendence does not arise with reference to the Absolute. For immanence implies the existence of an Other in which the Absolute is immanent. But the Absolute represents the totality of being and there is nothing other than it. The Absolute is in this world in the sense that the world is only an actualisation of one possibility of the Absolute and yet there is much in the Absolute beyond this possibility which is in process of realisation.

God is the Absolute with reference to this possibility of which He is the source and creator. Yet at any moment God transcends the cosmic process with its whole contents of space and time. He transcends the order of nature and history until His being is fully manifested. When that moment arises, the word becomes flesh, the whole world is saved and the historical process terminates. Until then,

God is partly in potentia, partly in act. This view is not pantheistic for the cosmic process is not a complete manifestation of the Absolute.

So far as the Absolute is concerned, the creation of the world makes no difference to it. It cannot add anything to or take away anything from the Absolute. All the sources of its being are found within itself. The world of change does not disturb the perfection of the Absolute. 'Though suns and universes would cease to be, Every existence would exist in thee' (Emily Brontë). We cannot say that the world follows from the nature of the Absolute even as the conclusion of the syllogism follows from the premise, as Spinoza would have us believe. The Absolute is the ground of the world only in the sense that a possibility of the Absolute is the logical prius of the world. The world would not be but for this possibility in the Absolute.

As to why this possibility arose and not any other, we have to answer that it is an expression of the freedom of the Absolute. It is not even necessary for the Absolute to express any of its possibilities. If this possibility is expressed, it is a free act of the Absolute. Hindu writers are inclined to look upon the act of creation more as the work of an artist than that of an artisan. It is līlā or free play. The world is the work of an artist whose works are worlds. His fertility is endless.

CONTEMPORARY INDIAN PHILOSOPHY, pp. 285–6

Even if with James we admit that philosophy is a matter of intuition and not intellect, absolutism becomes justified. We are led to it, whether we take our stand on the vital life and faith of the mystics or the certainties of the understanding.

REIGN OF RELIGION IN CONTEMPORARY PHILOSOPHY, p. 284

THE ABSOLUTE AND THE WORLD

There are aspects in religious experience, such as the sense of rest and fulfilment, of eternity and completeness, which require the conception of a being whose nature is not exhausted by the cosmic process, which possesses an allfulness of reality which our world only faintly shadows. This side of religious experience demands the conception of the supreme as self-existence, infinity, freedom, absolute light and absolute beatitude. On the other hand there are features of our religious experience which require us to look upon God as a self-determining principle manifested in a temporal development, with wisdom, love and goodness as his attributes. From this point of view God is a personal being with whom we can enter into personal relationship. Practical religion presupposes a God who looks into our hearts, knows our tribulations and helps us in our need. The reality of prayer and sacrifice is affirmed by the religious life of mankind. It assumes the reality of a concrete being who influences our life. To leave the Absolute in abstract isolation dwelling in Epicurean felicity is to reduce it to an ornamental figurehead who lends an atmosphere to an essentially agnostic view of the cosmic process. The permanent reality beyond the transient world of struggle and discord is also here and in everything. In religious experience itself there is no conflict. The supreme satisfies both sets of needs. But for philosophy of religion, the central problem is to reconcile the apparently conflicting views of the supreme as eternally complete and of the supreme as the self-determining principle manifesting in the temporal process.

CONTEMPORARY INDIAN PHILOSOPHY, pp. 280–1

While the character of God as personal love meets certain religious needs, there are others which are not fulfilled by it. In the highest spiritual experience we have the sense of rest and fulfilment, of eternity and completeness. These needs provoked from the beginning of human reflection conceptions of the Absolute as pure and passionless being which transcends the restless turmoil of the cosmic life. If God is bound up with the world, subject to the category of time, if his work is limited by the freedom of man and the conditions of existence, however infinite he may be in the quality of his life, in power, knowledge and righteousness, he is but an expression of the Absolute. But man wants to know the truth of things in itself, in the beginning—nay, before time and before plurality, the one 'breathing breathless,' as the Ṛg-Veda has it, the pure, alone and unmanifest, nothing and all things, that which transcends any definite form of expression, and yet is the basis of all expression, the one in whom all is found and yet all is lost. The great problem of the philosophy of religion has been the reconciliation of the character of the Absolute as in a sense eternally complete with the character of God as a self-determining principle manifested in a temporal development which includes nature and man.

AN IDEALIST VIEW OF LIFE, pp. 342–3

As a matter of fact, belief in a cosmic spirit which is friendly to us is the verdict of the religious consciousness.

REIGN OF RELIGION IN CONTEMPORARY PHILOSOPHY, p. 283

THE PERSONAL GOD

THE ideal of logic compels us to assume the reality of a perfect subject, to whom all existence is related as an object. Truth as systematic harmony means the reality of a divine experience. That events are interconnected in a system is the assumption of common sense and science, which is increasingly confirmed by experience, though never realised in its entirety. For there is much in the world which never directly enters into our experience. We seem to know much, though even in this limited region our knowledge is imperfect. Only a complete apprehension of reality as a whole can justify the hypothesis that God is and he is the creator of all.

INDIAN PHILOSOPHY, II, p. 542

God has no imperfections, no unfulfilled desires. The attribution of any motive (prayojana) to God conflicts with his all-sufficiency. If the world issued for some purpose or expressed some desire or fulfilled some want, then it would betray a sense of need and incompleteness in the Supreme. If he created with no definite aim, then his acts would be no better than a child's. If God were the sole cause the whole effect should have been present at once; but, as a matter of fact, we have a slowly unfolding growth which seems to indicate different causes for different stages. It is said in reply that action is not necessarily determined from without. It may be determined by motives intrinsic to the activity itself. So it is said that 'the activity of the Lord may be supposed to be mere sport (līlā) proceeding from his own nature, without reference to any purpose.' The creative activity of Īśvara is the undesired overflow of his perfection, which cannot rest sterilely in itself. The conception of līlā conveys a number of suggestions. The act of creation is not motived by any selfish interest. It is the spontaneous overflow of God's nature (svabhāva), even as it is the nature of man to breathe in and out. God cannot help creating. The work of the world is not the result of chance or thoughtlessness, but is simply the outcome of God's nature. Out of the fullness of his joy, God scatters abroad life and power.

INDIAN PHILOSOPHY, II, pp. 550–1

We cannot worship the Absolute whom no one hath seen or can see, who dwelleth in the light that no man can approach unto. The formless (nirākāram) Absolute is conceived as formed (ākāravat) for the purposes of worship. Worship of God is not a deliberate alliance with falsehood, since God is the form in which alone the Absolute can be pictured by the finite mind. The highest reality appears to the individual, who has not felt its oneness with his own nature, as possessing a number of perfections. The conception of a personal God is the fusion of the highest logical truth with the deepest religious conviction. This personal God is an object of genuine worship and reverence, and not a non-ethical deity indifferent to man's needs and fears. He is regarded as creator, governor and judge of the universe, possessing the qualities of power and justice, righteousness and mercy, omnipresence, omnipotence and omniscience. Holiness of character and moral beauty are prominent aspects of Śaṁkara's God. He is set over against the human soul, who stands to him in the relation of a beloved to a lover, a servant to a master, a son to a father, and a friend to a friend. The severity of metaphysical abstraction relaxes when Śaṁkara dwells on the variety of the divine qualities by which the eternal draws to himself the spirits of the children he has made. Religion for Śaṁkara is not doctrine or ceremony, but life and experience. It starts with the soul's sense of the infinite and ends with its becoming the infinite. Sākṣātkāra, or intuition of reality, is the end of religion. True bhakti is seeking after one's own real nature.

INDIAN PHILOSOPHY, II, p. 649

Only in the experience of the greatest contemplatives do we have the pure apprehension of the Absolute, the utter surrender of the creature to the Uncreated Spirit. The use of symbols and images is forced on us by our nature. Our thinking and feeling are intimately related to the world of things in which we live. By reference to things that are seen we give concrete form to the intuition of the reality that is unseen. Symbolism is an essential part of human life, the only possible response of a creature conditioned by time and space to the timeless and spaceless reality. Whether we pin our faith to stocks and stones or abstract thoughts and notions we are using concrete symbols which are impoverishments of the Supreme. In the fetish we have in a crude form the reinforcement of beliefs by the use of symbolic objects, and it persists even in the highest forms of faith. The highest symbols are only symbols, signs of an enduring reality which is larger than man's conception or picture of it.

EASTERN RELIGIONS AND WESTERN THOUGHT, pp. 317–18

LIFE AND EVOLUTION

When we pass to organic nature a new principle comes before us, the power of life immanent in certain things, by which they are able to realise a state of greater perfection, the power of realising an ideal. A stone does not live, since it has no tendency to become perfect, no inward inclination or strength to turn itself into a pillar or a statue. A plant, however, lives. If placed in suitable conditions, it has the power to grow, put forth leaf and blossom, flower and fruit. The animal, again, is capable of a fuller life than the plant. It sees, hears and feels, and also knows vaguely what it is about. Not only does it thrive in favourable conditions, but it goes out to find those conditions. It moves on purpose, while the plant does not. The human being lives a much higher life. He is what Śaṁkara calls a vyutpannacitta, a reflective being, with understanding and will. He has the growing power of the plant, the moving and the sensing powers of the animal, as well as the power to pierce behind the veil, discriminate the eternal from the non-eternal, and choose between good and evil. Men who realise their ambition are the gods. Thus under organic nature we find four classes of beings, gods, men, animals and plants. In the spirit of the Upaniṣads, Śaṁkara admits that plants are places of enjoyment and possess living souls, which have entered into them in consequence of impure deeds. Though they are insensible of enjoyment and suffering, they are said to be atoning for the deeds of their past existence. For Śaṁkara generally recognises three kinds of embodied souls, gods to whom is assigned a condition of infinite enjoyment, men whose lot is a mixed one of happiness and misery, and animals whose share is infinite suffering. In their embodied condition the souls exist together with the vital forces and subtle bodies, and, until they are liberated, these cling to them. The souls are said to be emanations from Brahman as the sparks are from fire; only they return into Brahman, while the sparks do not get back to fire.

INDIAN PHILOSOPHY, II, pp. 593–4

Whether we believe with the Upaniṣads in one universal spirit, or with the Śaṁkhya system in an infinite plurality of spirits, the nature of the spirit is conceived as unchanging and unchangeable. But ethical training implies the possibility of change. Man is not divine, but has to become divine. His divine status is something to be built up by good thoughts, good words, and good deeds. He is a concrete, living, striving creature. To tell him that there is a transcendental consciousness where scepticism and relativity are defeated from all eternity is not of much comfort. It is the concrete man, not the transcendental self, that has to acquire morality. The proposition that there is no permanent unchanging self in persons or things (sarvam anātmam) is not a speculative theory, or a sentimental outburst on the transitoriness of the world, but the basis of all ethics. We have to build the self by effort and discipline. The self is something which evolves and grows, something to be achieved and built up by pain and labour, and not something given to be passively accepted and enjoyed. The ego consists of the feelings that burn us, of the passions we brood over, of the desires that haunt us and of the decisions we make. These are the things that give life its dramatic character. There is nothing absolute and permanent in them. That is why we can become something different from what we are. The reality of the person is in the creative will. When we deny the clamour of emotions, stay the stream of things, silence the appetites of the body, we feel the power of self within our own being. Again, the delusion of self leads man to strive to profit himself and injure others. The passionate sense of egoism is the root of the world's unhappiness. To be egoistic is to be like a rudimentary creature that has grown no eyes. It is to be blind to the reality of other persons. We begin to grow only when we break down our clinging to the envelopes of the body and mind and realise that we have our roots in a state which is untouched by the familiar dimensions of this world. Detachment from ego means a gentler, profounder, sympathy with all sentient creation. It is the recovery of wholeness, of an ordered nature in harmony with the cosmos.

DHAMMAPADA, pp. 30–2

EVIL

THE moral argument that the context of things is adapted to the soul of man and shows the workmanship of a benevolent God is quite unsatisfactory. However the matter be turned, in a real world the responsibility for sin and evil falls on God. If, to relieve him of the authorship of evil, we accept something like the mythology of Persia and make Satan responsible for it, then the oneness of God disappears and we reinstate a dualism between God and Satan. Again, if the soul is a part of God, God must feel the pain of the soul also, even as, when one member of the body suffers, the whole body suffers with it. It follows that the sufferings of God are much greater than those of the individual souls, and it is better for us to remain self-enclosed individuals with our limited sufferings than rise to the level of God and take upon ourselves the burden of the whole world.

INDIAN PHILOSOPHY, II, p. 544

INDIAN THOUGHT

General Characteristics

FATE called India to a spot where nature was free with her gifts and every prospect was pleasing. The Himalayas with their immense range and elevation on one side and the sea on the others helped to keep India free from invasion for a long time. Bounteous nature yielded abundant food, and man was relieved of the toil and struggle for existence. The Indian never felt that the world was a field of battle where men struggled for power, wealth and domination. When we do not need to waste our energies on problems of life on earth, exploiting nature and controlling the forces of the world, we begin to think of the higher life, how to live more perfectly in the spirit. Perhaps an enervating climate inclined the Indian to rest and retirement. The huge forests with their wide leafy avenues afforded great opportunities for the devout soul to wander peacefully through them, dream strange dreams and burst forth into joyous songs. World-weary men go out on pilgrimages to these scenes of nature, acquire inward peace, listening to the rush of winds and torrents, the music of birds and leaves, and return whole of heart and fresh in spirit. It was in the āśramas and tapovanas or forest hermitages that the thinking men of India meditated on the deeper problems of existence. The security of life, the wealth of natural resources, the freedom from worry, the detachment from the cares of existence, and the absence of a tyrannous practical interest, stimulated the higher life of India, with the result that we find from the beginnings of history an impatience of spirit, a love of wisdom and a passion for the saner pursuits of the mind.

Helped by natural conditions, and provided with the intellectual scope to think out the implications of things, the Indian escaped the doom which Plato pronounced to be the worst of all, viz. the hatred of reason. 'Let us above all things take heed,' says he in the 'Phaedo,' 'that one misfortune does not befall us. Let us not become misologues as some people become misanthropes; for no greater evil can befall men than to become haters of reason.' The pleasure of understanding is one of the purest available to man, and the passion of the Indian for it burns in the bright flame of the mind.

INDIAN PHILOSOPHY, I, pp. 21–2

Reverence for the past is another national trait. There is a certain doggedness of temperament, a stubborn loyalty to lose nothing in the long march of the ages. When confronted with new cultures or sudden extensions of knowledge, the Indian does not yield to the temptations of the hour, but holds fast to his traditional faith, importing as much as possible of the new into the old. This conservative liberalism is the secret of the success of Indian culture and civilisation. Of the great civilisations of the world, hoary with age, only the Indian still survives. The magnificence of the Egyptian civilisation can be learnt only from the reports of the archaeologists and the readings of the hieroglyphics; the Babylonian Empire, with its marvels of scientific irrigation and engineering skill, is to-day nothing more than a heap of ruins; the great Roman culture, with its political institutions and ideals of law and equality, is, to a large extent, a thing of the past. The Indian civilisation, which even at the lowest estimate is 4,000 years old, still survives in its essential features. Her civilisation, dating back to the period of the Vedas, is young and old at the same time. She has been renewing her youth whenever the course of history demanded it. When a change occurs, it is not consciously felt to be a change. It is achieved, and all the time it professes to be only a new name for an old way of thinking. In the Ṛg-veda we shall see how the religious consciousness of the Aryan invaders takes note of the conceptions of the people of the soil. In the Atharva Veda we find that the vaguer cosmic deities are added to the gods of the sky and sun, fire and wind, worshipped by the Aryan peoples from the Ganges to the Hellespont. The Upaniṣads are regarded as a revival or rather a realisation of something found already in the Vedic hymns. The Bhagavadgītā professes to sum up the teachings of the Upaniṣads. We have in the epics the meeting-point of the religious conceptions of the highest import with the early nature-worship. To respect the spirit of reverence in man for the ancient makes for the success of the new. The old spirit is maintained, though not the old forms. This tendency to preserve the type has led to the fashionable remark that India is immobile. The mind of man never stands still, though it admits of no absolute breach with the past.

This respect for the past has produced a regular continuity in Indian thought, where the ages are bound each to each by natural piety. The Hindu culture is a product of ages of change wrought by hundreds of generations, of which some are long, stale and sad, and others short, quick and joyous, where each has added something of quality to the great rich tradition which is yet alive, though it bears within it the marks of the dead past. The career of Indian philosophy has been compared to the course of a stream which, tumbling joyfully from its source among the northern mountain-tops, rushes through the shadowy valleys and plains, catching the lesser streams in its imperious current, till it sweeps increased to majesty and serene power through the lands and peoples whose fortunes it affects, bearing a thousand ships on its bosom. Who knows whether and when this mighty stream which yet flows on with tumult and rejoicing will pass into the ocean, the father of all streams?

INDIAN PHILOSOPHY, I, pp. 46–7

The charge of unprogressiveness or stationariness holds when we reach the stage after the first great commentators. The hand of the past grew heavy, initiative was curbed, and the work of the scholastics, comparable to that of the medieval schoolmen, with the same reverence for authority and tradition and the same intrusion of theological prejudice, began. The Indian philosopher could have done better with greater freedom. To continue the living development of philosophy, to keep the current of creative energy flowing, contact with the living movements of the world capable of promoting real freedom of thought is necessary. Perhaps the philosophy of India, which lost its strength and vigour when her political fortunes met with defeat, may derive fresh inspiration and a new impulse from the era just dawning upon her. If the Indian thinkers combine a love of what is old with a thirst for what is true, Indian philosophy may yet have a future as glorious as its past.

INDIAN PHILOSOPHY, I, p. 53

Beneath the formalism of ceremonial worship there was at work a spirit of true religion and morality, from which the heart of man obtained satisfaction. It is this ethical basis which has helped the Brahmanical religion with all its weaknesses to endure so long. Side by side with its insistence on the outer, there was also the emphasis on inner purity. Truth, godliness, honour to parents, kindness to animals, love of man, abstinence from theft, murder and adultery, were inculcated as the essentials of a good life.

INDIAN PHILOSOPHY, I, p. 132

Ṛg-Veda

The process of god-making in the factory of man's mind cannot be seen so clearly anywhere else as in the Ṛg-Veda. We have in it the freshness and splendour of the morning of man's mind still undulled by past custom or fixed routine. There is no such thing as a beginning in the history of ideas, and we have to start somewhere. We may begin with the identification of the Vedic gods in some of their aspects with certain forces of nature, and point out how they were gradually raised to moral and superhuman beings. The earliest seers of the Vedic hymns delighted in sights of nature in their own simple unconscious way. Being essentially of a poetic temperament, they saw the things of nature with such intensity of feeling and force of imagination that the things became suffused with souls. They knew what it was to love nature, and be lost in the wonders of dawn and sunrise, those mysterious processes which effect a meeting of the soul and nature. To them nature was a living presence with which they could hold communion. Some glorious aspects of nature became the windows of heaven, through which the divine looked down upon the godless earth. The moon and the stars, the sea and the sky, the dawn and the nightfall were regarded as divine. This worship of nature as such is the earliest form of Vedic religion.

INDIAN PHILOSOPHY, I, p. 73

Upaniṣads

The aim of the Upaniṣads is not so much to reach philosophical truth as to bring peace and freedom to the anxious human spirit. Tentative solutions of metaphysical questions are put forth in the form of dialogues and disputations, though the Upaniṣads are essentially the outpourings or poetic deliverances of philosophically tempered minds in the face of the facts of life. They express the restlessness and striving of the human mind to grasp the true nature of reality. Not being systematic philosophy, or the production of a single author, or even of the same age, they contain much that is inconsistent and unscientific; but if that were all, we cannot justify the study of the Upaniṣads. They set forth fundamental conceptions which are sound and satisfactory, and these constitute the means by which their own innocent errors, which through exclusive emphasis have been exaggerated into fallacious philosophies, can be corrected. Notwithstanding the variety of authorship and the period of time covered by the composition of these half-poetical and half-philosophical treatises, there is a unity of purpose, a vivid sense of spiritual reality in them all, which become clear and distinct as we descend the stream of time. They reveal to us the wealth of the reflective religious mind of the times. In the domain of intuitive philosophy their achievement is a considerable one. Nothing that went before them for compass and power, for suggestiveness and satisfaction, can stand comparison with them. Their philosophy and religion have satisfied some of the greatest thinkers and intensely spiritual souls.

INDIAN PHILOSOPHY, I, pp. 138–9

Karma

The law of karma is the counterpart in the moral world of the physical law of uniformity. It is the law of the conservation of moral energy. The vision of law and order is revealed in the Ṛta of the Ṛg-Veda. According to the principle of karma there is nothing uncertain or capricious in the moral world. We reap what we sow. The good seed brings a harvest of good, the evil of evil. Every little action has its effect on character. Man knows that some of the tendencies to action which now exist in him are the result of conscious or intelligent choice on his part. Conscious actions tend to become unconscious habits, and not unnaturally the unconscious tendencies we find in ourselves were regarded as the result of past conscious actions. We cannot arrest the process of moral evolution any more than we can stay the sweep of the tides or the course of the stars. The attempt to overleap the law of karma is as futile as the attempt to leap over one's shadow. It is the psychological principle that our life carries within it a record that time cannot blur or death erase.

INDIAN PHILOSOPHY, I, pp. 244–5

Man is not a mere product of nature. He is mightier than his karma. If the law is all, then there is no real freedom possible. Man's life is not the working of merely mechanical relations. There are different levels—the mechanical, the vital, the sentient, the intellectual and the spiritual—these currents cross and recross and interpenetrate each other. The law of karma, which rules the lower nature of man, has nothing to do with the spiritual in him. The infinite in man helps him to transcend the limitations of the finite. The essence of spirit is freedom. By its exercise man can check and control his natural impulses. That is why his life is something more than a succession of mechanically determined states. His acts to be free must not be expressive of the mere force of habit or shock of circumstance, but of the freedom of the inner soul. The spiritual nature is the basis of his initiative and endeavour. The mechanical part is under constraint. Were man merely the sum of natural conditions, he would be completely subject to the law of karma. But there is a soul in him which is the master. Nothing external can compel it. We are sure that the material forces of the world must bend to the spiritual rule, and so can the law of karma be subjected to the freedom of spirit.

INDIAN PHILOSOPHY, I, p. 246

Schools

An age stricken with a growing sense of moral weakness is eager to clutch at any spiritual stay. We have the materialists with their insistence on the world of sense, the Buddhists with their valuable psychological teaching and high ethics. While there were some who clung to the Vedas with the desperation of the drowning man, the reformers gave themselves over to the moral task of living clean lives and doing good work, deliberately refusing to speculate about the possibility of the beyond. Ascetics, Tīrthakaras or ford-makers claimed to be founders of new paths. Gautama and Vardhamāna were the most prominent reformers. Buddhist books mention other heretical teachers: Sañjaya the sceptic, who repudiated all knowledge of self and limited his inquiries to the question of the attainment of peace; Ajita Keśakambalin the materialist, who rejected all knowledge by insight and resolved man into the four elements which dispersed at death; Pūraṇa Kāśyapa the indifferentist, who refused to acknowledge moral distinctions and adopted the view of non-causation or fortuitous origin and passivity of soul; Maskarin Gosāla the fatalist, who held that man had no power over life or death, and who believed that all things were living jīvas in process of constant change determined by their immanent energy till they attained perfection; and Kakuḍa Kātyāyana, who maintained the qualitative distinctness of the elements of being, earth, water, fire, air, space and soul, with pleasure and pain as principles of change, making and unmaking individuals. Numberless teachers rose in different parts of the country announcing the good news of the secret of deliverance.

INDIAN PHILOSOPHY, I, pp. 274–5

Buddhism

In the age of Buddha men of keen intellect and deep feeling were asking, 'What does all this weary round of existence mean?' and Buddha addressed his appeal to the men who were longing for a way of escape, a resort to nirvāṇa, where the wicked cease from troubling and the weary are at rest. Insistence on suffering is not peculiar to Buddhism, though Buddha emphasised it overmuch. In the whole history of thought no one has painted the misery of human existence in blacker colours and with more feeling than Buddha. The melancholy foreshadowed in the Upaniṣads occupies the central place here. Possibly the ascetic ideals of an unreasoned exaltation of poverty, glorification of self-sacrifice, and an obsession of renunciation cast a hypnotic spell over Buddha's mind. To make people long for escape from this world, its blackness is a little overdrawn. We may try all we can to spread comfort and happiness and suppress all social injustice, yet man will not have satisfaction.

INDIAN PHILOSOPHY, I, pp. 362–3

If pessimism means that life on earth is not worth living unless it be in purity and detachment, then Buddhism is pessimism. If it means that it is best to be done with life on earth for there is bliss beyond, then Buddhism is pessimism. But this is not true pessimism. A system is pessimistic if it stifles all hope and declares 'to live on earth is weariness and there is no bliss beyond.' Some forms of

Buddhism do declare this and are justly called pessimistic. So far as the early teaching of Buddha is concerned, it is not that. It is true that it considers life to be an unending succession of torments, but it believes in the liberating power of ethical discipline and the perfectibility of human nature. Again, though the suffering of creation weighs upon Buddha's mind, it does not seem to be purposeless. Desire is there to impel us to the supreme effort to abandon all desire. Each man has his own burden to bear, and every heart knows its own bitterness, and yet through it all goodness grows and progress becomes perfection. The world with all its suffering seems adapted to the growth of goodness. Buddha does not preach the mere worthlessness of life or resignation to an inevitable doom. His is not a doctrine of despair. He asks us to revolt against evil and attain a life of a finer quality, an ārhata state.

INDIAN PHILOSOPHY, I, p. 365

A wonderful philosophy of dynamism was formulated by Buddha 2,500 years ago, a philosophy which is being re-created for us by the discoveries of modern science and the adventures of modern thought. The electro-magnetic theory of matter has brought about a revolution in the general concept of the nature of physical reality. It is no more static stuff but radiant energy. An analogous change has pervaded the world of psychology, and the title of a recent book by M. Bergson, *Mind Energy*, indicates the change in the theory of psychical reality. Impressed by the transitoriness of objects, the ceaseless mutation and transformation of things, Buddha formulated a philosophy of change. He reduces substances, souls, monads, things to forces, movements, sequences and processes, and adopts a dynamic conception of reality. Life is nothing but a series of manifestations of becomings and extinctions. It is a stream of becoming. The world of sense and science is from moment to moment. It is a recurring rotation of birth and death. Whatever be the duration of any state of being, as brief as a flash of lightning or as long as a millennium, yet all is becoming. All things change. All schools of Buddhism agree that there is nothing human or divine that is permanent. Buddha gives us a discourse on fire to indicate the ceaseless flux of becoming called the world.

INDIAN PHILOSOPHY, I, pp. 367–8

In all individuals, without exception, the relation of the component parts to one another is ever changing. It is never the same for two consecutive moments. Man is a living continuous complex, which does not remain the same for two moments, and yet continues in an endless number of existences without being completely different from itself. While both mind and body are in ceaseless change, impermanence is more marked and the flow more rapid in mind than in body, so that if we wish to speak of anything as permanent it must be rather of body than of mind.

INDIAN PHILOSOPHY, I, p. 383

Buddha, more a teacher than a saviour, helps us to see the truth. He does not imagine a world-maker far back in the ages, beginning the series of saṁsāra. The flow of the world has no other cause beside itself. To him the cosmological argument had no force. Enough if we know how things happen. We need not go behind the order of the world. Though an explanation by antecedent conditions is no final truth, still to man nothing more is open. A first cause which is itself uncaused seems to be self-contradictory. The necessity of conceiving every cause as effect which has its cause in a preceding one makes the conception of an uncaused cause absolutely unthinkable. Similarly, the teleological argument is untenable in view of the obvious imperfection of the world. The world seems to be an ingenious contrivance for inflicting suffering. Nothing could be more elaborate and masterly in its perfection than this scheme of pain. A perfect Creator cannot be the author of this imperfect world. Neither a benevolent God nor caprice, but a law which works with a fatal logic, is the truth of things. Buddha would agree with Spinoza in the view that the world is neither good nor bad, neither heartless nor irrational, neither perfect nor beautiful. It is man's anthropomorphism that makes him look upon the cosmic process as a sort of human activity. Nature obeys no laws imposed from without. We have only necessities in nature.

INDIAN PHILOSOPHY, I, pp. 455–6

Nirvāṇa is an eternal condition of being, for it is not a saṁskāra, or what is made or put together, which is impermanent. It continues while its expression changes. This is what lies behind the skandhas, which are subject to birth and decay. The illusion of becoming is founded on the reality of nirvāṇa. Buddha does not attempt to define it, since it is the root principle of all, and so is indefinable. It is said that in nirvāṇa, which is compared to deep sleep, the soul loses its individuality and lapses into the objective whole. According to the view emphasised in later Mahāyāna works, what is is the bhavāṅga, or the stream of being. The wind of ignorance blows over it and stirs its equable flow, causing vibrations in the ocean of existence. The sleeping soul is wakened and its calm unfettered course is arrested. It wakes up, thinks, builds an individuality and isolates itself from the stream of being. In deep sleep these barriers are broken. Nirvāṇa is getting back into the stream of being and resuming the uninterrupted flow. Even as no thought-waves perturb the stream of being when a man sleeps, so also in nirvāṇa do we have peaceful rest. Nirvāṇa is neither annihilation nor existence as we conceive it, but is becoming one with the eternal reality, which Buddha does not explicitly admit. Only since it is beyond the horizon of human thought we are obliged to employ negative terms to describe it. It is a condition transcending subject-object relations. In it there is no trace of self-consciousness. It is a state of activity which is not subject to causality, for it is unconditioned freedom. It is a state real and enduring, though not existent in the world of time and space. The psalms of the elders and the nuns are full of eloquent descriptions of the deep joy and the immortal delight of nirvāṇa surpassing all description. The individual consciousness enters into a state where all relative existence is dissolved. It is the silent beyond. In one sense it is self-extinction, in another absolute freedom. It is the fading of the star in the brilliant rise of the sun or the melting of the white cloud in the summer air. To think that nirvāṇa is annihilation is according to Buddha 'a wicked heresy.'

INDIAN PHILOSOPHY, I, pp. 449–50

Identity of objects is only another name for continuity of becoming. A child—a boy—a youth—a man—an old man are one. The seed and the tree are one. The banyan tree a thousand years old is one and the same plant with the seed out of which it has grown. It is the succession that gives the appearance of an unbroken identity. Though the substance of our bodies as well as the constitution of our souls changes from moment to moment, still we say it is the same old thing or the same old man. A thing is only a series of states of which the first is said to be the cause of the second, for they seem to be of the same nature. The seeming identity from moment to moment consists in a continuity of moments which we may call the continuity of an ever-changing identity. The world is a number of accidents ever changing and being renewed at every breath and each moment disappearing, only to be replaced by a similar set. In consequence of this rapid succession, the spectator is deceived into the belief that the universe is a permanent existence, even as a glowing stick whirled round produces the appearance of a complete circle. A useful convention makes us give names and forms to the individual. The identity of name and form is no evidence of the identity of the inner reality. Again, we are naturally led to imagine a permanent core, but it is an abstraction of thinking. We say it rains, while there is no 'it' at all. There is nothing but movement, no doer but deed, nothing else but a becoming.

INDIAN PHILOSOPHY, I, p. 370

No other independent ethics gives us a more thrilling message of universal benevolence. At a time when bloody sacrifices were not yet out of fashion, the teaching of mercy to all creation had a tremendous effect. His opposition to ceremonialism contributed largely to recommend his doctrine to the masses. The sublime grandeur of Buddha's teaching may be gathered from the following utterances of his: 'Never in this world does hatred cease by hatred—hatred ceases by love.' 'Victory breeds hatred, for the conquered is unhappy.' 'One may conquer a thousand men in battle, but he who conquers himself is the greatest victor.' 'Let a man overcome anger by kindness, evil by good.' 'Not by birth, but by his conduct alone, does a man become a low caste or a Brahmin.' 'Hide your good deeds and confess before the world the sins you have committed.' 'Who would willingly use hard speech to those who have done a sinful deed, strewing salt, as it were, upon the wound of their fault?' No voice like Buddha's ever thundered into our ears the majesty of the good. It is the flaming ideal of righteousness that helped Buddhism to succeed as a religion. The missionary spirit contributed considerably to the spread of the gospel. Buddha bade his disciples: 'Go into all lands and preach this gospel. Tell them that the poor and the lowly, the rich and the high, are all one, and that all castes unite in this religion as do the rivers in the sea.' Buddhism succeeded so well because it was a religion of love, giving voice to all the inarticulate forces which were working against the established order and the ceremonial religion, addressing itself to the poor, the lowly and the disinherited.

INDIAN PHILOSOPHY, I, pp. 474–5

The supremacy of the ethical is the clue to the teaching of Buddha. It is clearly visible in his life and thought. The opening words of his first sermon to the five monks relate to the avoiding of the extremes of self-indulgence, which is low and vulgar, and self-mortification, which is crazy and fantastic. After warning the ascetics regarding the exaggerated value they attribute to austerities, Buddha defines the middle way or the eightfold path. And only later does he enunciate the four truths of the nature of suffering, its origin, its cessation and the method of reaching it. His sixth convert, Yasa, is approached in a slightly different way, probably because he was a layman. After treating of moral duties, desires and their renunciation, the four truths are enunciated. 'Even as the great ocean has only one taste, the taste of salt, so has this doctrine and discipline only one taste, the taste of nirvāṇa.' Buddha discouraged all metaphysical speculation about the motive and meaning of the universe, since such questions seemed to be irrelevant to his scheme of salvation. Aśoka's rock edicts, which are the earliest indication of Buddha's teaching, are eminently practical in character.

HIBBERT JOURNAL, vol. 32, 1933-4, p. 345.

Buddha is indifferent to the question of a supreme personal God. He is aware of the actual implications of such a conception for ethical life. For Buddha religion is not a matter of doctrines or dogmas, ceremonies or sacraments, but a state of the mind. It is to devote oneself with all one's thought, strength and heart to the good life. To be religious is to believe in the interdependence of the spiritual and ordinary life. The essence of his creed is not so much 'I believe' as 'I give myself.' The acceptance of a creed is easy; the pursuit of a life is hard. The theistic worshippers of Buddha's day were inclined to cast their burdens on providence and take refuge in God. They tried to escape from effort by expecting dramatic happenings Buddha insisted on internal effort and intense striving. What we make of our lives cannot be undone. It is erroneous to imagine that it matters little what we do in this life, so long as we do not forget to remember God's name in the last moments of life. Religion is here or nowhere, now or never. It is a constant struggle with the forces of evil. In this battle one has to rely on the strength of one's personality. By means of meditation one draws the power of the universe into oneself and brings the soul into relation with the unseen. Buddha, at any rate, did not, in my opinion, accept the view of a personal God, since such a belief tended to indolence and hypocrisy. Here again it is the ethical interest that is responsible for his attitude.

HIBBERT JOURNAL, vol. 32, 1933–4, p. 347

Sariputta tells Yamaka that, even as we cannot understand the mystery of personality, we cannot understand the state of a saint's being after death. Thought reaches here a deep mystery, on the solution of which it should not insist. In other words, it is not annihilation, utter and complete. In the realm of the changing itself there must be contained, veiled perhaps, but still present, an element which bears in itself the pledge of eternal life, stretching out beyond origination and decease. There is a life in us which is non-successive, non-extended, and our destiny is to make it fully real. If we did not have it, we would not be dissatisfied with the finite. If the universe were a simple succession and the human individual nothing more than a changing complex, there could not be any dissatisfaction with the finite and the changing. Even for consciousness of change, there must be at the back of all change an element of permanence. The teaching of non-self is a denying of what people generally mistake for self. It is not, however, to deny altogether the reality of self. There is in us a thirst for the ultimates, a quest for the eternal, and it is not satisfied by the things of the world. For the world in which we wander is not our home. Things seen and temporal imply things unseen and eternal. We judge things as fleeting because we have a consciousness of the enduring.

HIBBERT JOURNAL, vol. 32, 1933–4, pp. 352–3

For the removal of ignorance a strict morality is essential. Śīla and prajña, good conduct and intuitive insight, are inseparably united. The Buddha does not speak of codes and conventions, laws and rites. The way to be happy is to have a good heart and mind which will show itself in good deeds. Simple goodness in spirit and deed is the basis of his religion. He detaches the perfect life from all connection with a deity or outside forces and teaches man that the best and the worst that can happen to him lie within his own power. We frequently hear him say: 'Come, disciples, lead a holy life for the extinction of sorrow.' The noble eight-fold path represents a ladder of perfection. The first step is right views, knowledge of the four truths, which is not to be confused with the gnosis, jñana of the Upaniṣads, or the faith of the theists. But so long as the truths are known only in the intellect they have no life. They must be discovered and proved by every man in the depths of his own being. The first step is an awakening, a summons to abandon a way by which we miss our truth and destiny. It is not a casual change of opinion, but a radical adjustment of nature which affects the very depths of the soul and leads to the second step of right aspirations towards renunciation, benevolence, and kindness. It is to resolve to renounce pleasures, to bear no malice, and do no harm. Right speech requires us to abstain from lying, slander, abuse, harsh words, and idle talk. Right action is to abstain from taking life, or taking what is not given, or from carnal excesses. Right livelihood is to abstain from any of the forbidden modes of living, which are those of a trader in weapons, slave-dealer, butcher, publican, or poison-seller. The Buddha forbade his monks ever to become soldiers. The eight-fold path is more than a code of morality. It is a way of life. Right effort consists in suppressing the rising of evil states, in eradicating those which have arisen, in stimulating good states and perfecting those which have come into being. It is the beginning of mental cultivation. The habit of self-observation is an effective way to deal with the underworld of the human mind, to root out evil desires and cravings, to maintain an equilibrium between the conscious mind and the other part of our equipment, the complicated psychic and physical apparatus. Man is false and deceitful not merely in relation to others, but to himself as well. We adopt ideas not always out of pure and disinterested motives, but through some kind of resentment or failure in life. We become vindictive and tyrannical because our pride has been wounded, or our love has been unrequited, or because we have had some humiliating physical deformity. The remarkable thing about man is that he often deceives himself. Many of us are machines most of the time. Our thoughts and feelings follow an habitual pattern. Through self-examination we attempt to break up automatisms, destroy the reliance of the mind on habitual props and discover the self. Sloth and torpor are as harmful to spiritual progress as evil desires. Right-mindfulness is to look on the body and the spirit in such a way as to remain self-possessed and mindful, overcoming both hankering and dejection. It is self-mastery by means of self-knowledge which allows nothing to be done mechanically or heedlessly. It is to see things under the aspect of eternity. Right contemplation takes the form of the four meditations. There is a curious impression that the Buddha's prescription for good life is the cessation of activity, desiring little and doing nothing. The resolve to win the saving truth, the efforts needful for its attainment, the lives spent in the practice of virtue, the unrelaxing tension of will maintained through constant temptation to aim at less than the highest, all rest on the certitude that the human will is capable of heroic endeavour and achievement. Meditation is an act of attention, an effort of will. It is not passive reverie, but intense striving, concentration of mind in which will and thought become fused. According to the Buddha's teaching each man will have to find salvation, in the last resort, alone and with his own will, and he needs all the will in the world for so formidable an effort. The general impression that the mystic experience is granted and not achieved is far from correct, except in the sense that all great moments of experience are in a measure given. The mystic is not so much passive as receptive. His life is one of strenuous discipline. Right contemplation is the end and the crown of the eight-fold path. When the mind and the senses are no longer active, when discursive thought ceases, we get the highest and purest state of the soul, when it enjoys the untrammelled bliss of its own nature. It is the substance of the highest life when ignorance and craving become extinct and insight and holiness take their place. It is peaceful contemplation and ecstatic rapture wrought by the mind for itself. It is the true and healthy life of the soul, in which we have a foretaste of a higher existence compared with which our ordinary life is sick and ailing. We have in it a sense of freedom, of knowledge, immediate and unbounded.

DHAMMAPADA, pp. 19–22

Mahāyāna and Hīnayāna

The arhat ideal is the distinguishing-mark of the Hīnayāna, which believes in the possibility of emancipation through one's own powers. The method is contemplation and meditation on the four truths. The Hīnayāna Buddhism is indefinite about the Buddhahood of those who reach arhatā, nor does it suggest that every creature may attain Buddhahood. We cannot help feeling that the ideal of the arhat, the perfect egoist, who is useless to others, is untrue to the real personality of Buddha, the man of pity and compassion, though the dependence on the saviour Buddha of the Mahāyāna faith is also untrue to the teaching of the original Buddha, however useful it may be. The Hīnayāna ideal may be justly summed up in the statement of Ibsen: 'There are actually moments when the whole history of the world appears to me like one great shipwreck, and the only important thing seems to be to save oneself.'

INDIAN PHILOSOPHY, I, pp. 586–7

The Hīnayāna, like the 'unshown way' of those who seek the 'Nirguṇa Brahman,' is exceeding hard; whereas the burden of the Mahāyāna is light, and does not require that a man should immediately renounce the world and all the affections of humanity. The manifestation of the body of the Law, says the Mahāyāna, is adapted to the various needs of the children of the Buddha; whereas the Hīnayāna is only of avail to those who have left their spiritual childhood far behind them.

INDIAN PHILOSOPHY, I, p. 591

The Hīnayāna protests against the Mahāyāna as an accommodation of the pure teaching to the necessities of human nature. Anyway, while it stands as an example to the world of realising the highest through knowledge, the Mahāyāna requires us to take part in the world, evolving new social and religious ideals. The absence of the supernatural and the consequent lack of any scope for imagination, the morbid way of solving the central problems of life, the reduction of nirvāṇa to extinction and ethical life to a monastic asceticism, made the Hīnayāna a religion for the thinking and the strong in spirit, while a new development had to arise for the emotional and the worshipful.

INDIAN PHILOSOPHY, I, p. 592

Hinduism

Hinduism developed an attitude of comprehensive charity instead of a fanatic faith in an inflexible creed. It accepted the multiplicity of aboriginal gods and others which originated, most of them, outside the Aryan tradition, and justified them all. It brought together into one whole all believers in God. Many sects professing many different beliefs live within the Hindu fold. Heresy-hunting, the favourite game of many religions, is singularly absent from Hinduism.

Hinduism is wholly free from the strange obsession of the Semitic faith that the acceptance of a particular religious metaphysic is necessary for salvation, and non-acceptance thereof is a heinous sin meriting eternal punishment in hell. Here and there outbursts of sectarian fanaticism are found recorded in the literature of the Hindus, which indicate the first effects of the conflicts, of the different groups brought together into the one fold; but the main note of Hinduism is one of respect and good will for other creeds.

HINDU VIEW OF LIFE, p. 37

Toleration is the homage which the finite mind pays to the inexhaustibility of the Infinite.

EASTERN RELIGIONS AND WESTERN THOUGHT, p. 317

As a result of this tolerant attitude, Hinduism itself has become a mosaic of almost all the types and stages of religious aspiration and endeavour. It has adapted itself with infinite grace to every human need and it has not shrunk from the acceptance of every aspect of God conceived by man, and yet preserved its unity by interpreting the different historical forms as modes, emanations, or aspects of the Supreme.

EASTERN RELIGIONS AND WESTERN THOUGHT, p. 313

Hinduism requires every man to think steadily on life's mystery until he reaches the highest revelation. While the lesser forms are tolerated in the interests of those who cannot suddenly transcend them, there is all through an insistence on the larger idea and the purer worship. Hinduism does not believe in forcing up the pace of development. When we give our higher experiences to those who cannot understand them we are in the position of those who can see and who impart the visual impressions to those born blind. Unless we open their spiritual eyes, they cannot see what the seers relate. So while Hinduism does not interfere with one's natural way of thinking, which depends on his moral and intellectual gifts, education and environment, it furthers his spiritual growth by lending a sympathetic and helping hand wherever he stands. While Hinduism hates the compulsory conscription of men into the house of truth, it insists on the development of one's intellectual conscience and sensibility to truth.

HINDU VIEW OF LIFE, p. 49

Indian culture is not racially exclusive, but has affected men of all races. It is international in feeling and intention. As the typical religion of India, Hinduism represents this spirit, the spirit that has such extraordinary vitality as to survive political and social changes. From the beginning of recorded history, Hinduism has borne witness to the sacred flame of spirit which must remain for ever, even while dynasties crash and empires tumble into ruins. It alone can give our civilisation a soul, and men and women a principle to live by.

RELIGION AND SOCIETY, p. 43

From the beginning of her history India has adored and idealised, not soldiers and statesmen, not men of science and leaders of industry, not even poets and philosophers, who influence the world by their deeds or by their words, but those rarer and more chastened spirits, whose greatness lies in what they are and not in what they do; men who have stamped infinity on the thought and life of the country, men who have added to the invisible forces of goodness in the world. To a world given over to the pursuit of power and pleasure, wealth and glory, they declare the reality of the unseen world and the call of the spiritual life. Their self-possession and self-command, their strange deep wisdom, their exquisite courtesy, their humility and gentleness of soul, their abounding humanity proclaim that the destiny of man is to know himself and thereby further the universal life of which he is an integral element.

HIBBERT JOURNAL, vol. 35, 1936–7, p. 26

The contemplative thinkers who transmit to their generation the delicacy of old forms, reverence for the past, the breath of history, the power to feel and understand the secure and the self-contained, as well as the visions of new things and vistas of a transformed age, men who know how to look upon tradition as something fluid and mobile, constantly modified and changed by the demands of life, are not among those who belong to the priestly profession to-day. The present class of priests, with rare exceptions, have lost their good breeding, kindliness and polish and have not gained in sureness of intellect, learning or adaptability. They know only that the disciple of tradition erects a barrier against radicalism and excessive individualism. They think that they are safeguarding the community against revolutionary change but are only fomenting it. If we pull off their masks, doubters stand revealed in many cases. They are not sure of what they preach and are mere opportunists by reason of a dumb gnawing despair whose nature they themselves do not understand. They are to some extent responsible for the prevalent spiritual sluggishness. They thrust formulas into our heads which we repeat mechanically, without any real knowledge of what they mean. A few ceremonies are observed more out of regard for our reputation or our relatives or as a matter of habit than out of any inward urge or sense of community. We are Hindus simply because of the legal framework of life and the individual feeling of security within which we live and have our being. Many of us have not the slightest idea of the true nature of religion, that hidden flame, which is more active among the young whose minds are in ferment. We can hear the call and the challenge of the youth for a new emphasis in religion, a new mankind. It is of the spirit of youth that it can never entirely despair of human nature. It will debase itself rather than cease to believe in its dream visions. It is convinced that the affliction that is visited on us is the return for our common failure.

CONTEMPORARY INDIAN PHILOSOPHY, pp. 259–60

The triumphs of this method of religious reform have been striking: no less so are its failures. After these many centuries, Hinduism, like the curate's egg, is good only in parts. It is admirable and abhorrent, saintly and savage, beautifully wise and dangerously silly, generous beyond measure and mean beyond all example. It is strange how long primitive superstitions will last, if we do not handle them roughly. When they were taken over by Hinduism, they were given added respectability. It is not easy to move men to quit their old ways, overcome indolence and inertia, and venture on new paths. Though the most revolting practices of cannibalism, polyandry, and human sacrifices were soon abolished, others, such as animal sacrifices, repugnant to our moral sentiments, still persist. While we may criticise the cheap assurance of reformers, they are morally a force to be greatly welcomed, for they have the quality of a faith that moves mountains. The Hindu method, being a democratic one, is more expensive and wasteful. Reform by consent is slower than reform by compulsion in religion as in politics, but it has the human touch. Life is a school of patience and 'charity suffereth long.' An extensive application of the principle of liberty, equality, and fraternity has made Hinduism the most elastic of all religions, the most capable of adapting itself to new conditions. It is less dependent on historical facts, is freer from authority. Its gods form no exclusive group. Its pantheon has stood wide open for the admission of new deities who are always naturalised as aspects of the Supreme godhead. The danger of the Hindu attitude is that what is may be accepted because it is, and progress may be infinitely delayed.

EASTERN RELIGIONS AND WESTERN THOUGHT, pp. 338–9

Religion expresses itself in and discloses its quality by the morality which it demands. While there is a good deal in Hindu religion and practice which merits just criticism, dark aspects of brutality, cruelty, violence, ignorance of nature, superstition and fear, in its essence the religion seemed to me to be quite sound. Its followers are carried along by a longing for the vision of God which has brought some of them to the verge of a holy perfection in which the perplexing dichotomy between the flesh and the spirit which men forever feel but never understand is overcome. Hindu culture is directed towards that which is transcendent and beyond. Its great achievements in times past were due to a high tension of the spirit to which our age has no parallel.

CONTEMPORARY INDIAN PHILOSOPHY, p. 258

One of the arguments of the conservatives is that truth is not affected by time. It cannot be superseded, any more than the beauty of the sunset or a mother's love for a child. Truth may be immutable, but the form in which it is embodied consists of elements which admit of change. We may take our spirit from the past, for the germinal ideas are yet vital, but the body and the pulse must be from the present. It is forgotten that religion, as it is to-day, is itself the product of ages of change; and there is no reason why its forms should not undergo fresh changes so long as the spirit demands it. It is possible to remain faithful to the letter and yet pervert the whole spirit. If the Hindu leaders of two thousand years ago, who had less learning and more light, could come on earth again after all these centuries, they would seldom find their true followers among those who have never deviated from the most literal interpretations of their views. To-day a great mass of accretions have accumulated, which are choking up the stream and the free life of spirit. To say that the dead forms, which have no vital truth to support them, are too ancient and venerable to be tampered with, only prolongs the suffering of the patient who is ailing from the poison generated by the putrid waste of the past. The conservative mind must open itself to the necessity of change. Since it is not sufficiently alive to this need, we find in the realm of philosophy a strange mixture of penetrating sagacity and unphilosophical confusion. The chief energies of the thinking Indians should be thrown into the problems of how to disentangle the old faith from its temporary accretions, how to bring religion into line with the spirit of science, how to meet and interpret the claims of temperament and individuality, how to organise the divergent influences on the basis of the ancient faith. But, unfortunately, some of the pariṣads are engaged not with these problems but those suited for the society of antiquarians. They have become the tilting-ground of the specialists. The religious education of the nation is not undertaken on broad lines. It is not seen that the spiritual inheritance cannot be any longer the monopoly of a favoured few. Ideas are forces, and they must be broadcasted, if the present ageing to death is to be averted. It would be indeed strange if the spirit of the Upaniṣads, the Gītā and the Dialogues of Buddha, that could touch the mind to such fine issues, should have lost its power over man. If, before it is too late, there is a reorganisation of national life, there is a future for Indian thought; and one cannot tell what flowers may yet bloom, what fruits may yet ripen on the hardy old trees.

INDIAN PHILOSOPHY, II, pp. 777–8

The Saṁkhya System

The Sāṁkhya description of the world in terms of one homogeneous substance, of which all things are but different configurations resulting from the different combinations of its ultimate constituents, has some resemblance to the materialist theory. Both the Sāṁkhya and materialism attempt to attain a more rational conception of the universe than the somewhat chaotic view which surface appearances leave on our minds. Both of them assert the ultimate reality of a primary substance which they regard as eternal, indestructible and ubiquitous. The multiplicity of heterogeneous things which we come across in our ordinary experience is traced to this single substance. But the prakṛti of the Sāṁkhya cannot be compared with matter pure and simple. The Sāṁkhya thinkers are aware of the incapacity of prakṛti to produce puruṣa as well as the incapacity of puruṣa to produce prakṛti. They admit, while the materialists do not, that the evolution of prakṛti is purposive, 'an arch where through gleams the untravelled world.' The prakṛti of the Sāṁkhya is not a material substance, nor is it a conscious entity, since purusa is carefully distinguished from it. It gives rise not only to the five elements of the material universe, but also to the psychical. It is the basis of all objective existence. The Sāṁkhya arrives at the conception, not from the side of science, but from that of metaphysics. The real in its fullness is distinguished into the unchanging subject, and the changing object and prakṛti is the basis of the latter, the world of becoming. It is the symbol of the never-resting, active world stress. It goes on acting unconsciously, without regard to any thought-out plan, working for ends which it does not understand.

INDIAN PHILOSOPHY, II, pp. 261–2

All organic beings have a principle of self-determination, to which the name of 'soul' is generally given. In the strict sense of the word, 'soul' belongs to every being that has life in it, and the different souls are fundamentally identical in nature. The differences are due to the physical organisations that obscure and thwart the life of the soul. The nature of the bodies in which the souls are incorporated accounts for their various degrees of obscuration. The souls cannot be referred to the same principle from which physical organisations spring. So the Sāṁkhya asserts the existence of puruṣas freed from all the accidents of finite life and lifted above time and change. There is the testimony of consciousness that, though the individual is in one aspect a particular finite being subject to all the accidents and changes of mortality, there is something in him which lifts him above them all. He is not the mind, life or body, but the informing and sustaining soul, silent peaceful, eternal, that possesses them. When the facts of the world are viewed from the epistemological point of view, we get a classification into subjects on the one side and objects on the other. The relation between any subject and any object is that of cognition or, more broadly, experience. The Sāṁkhya regards the knower as puruṣa and the known as prakṛti.

INDIAN PHILOSOPHY, II, pp. 279–80

The doctrine of the guṇas has great ethical significance. The beings of the world are classified according to the preponderance of the different guṇas in them. In the devas the sattva element predominates, while the rajas and the tamas are reduced. In man the tamas element is reduced to a less extent than in the devas. In the animal world the sattva is reduced considerably. In the vegetable kingdom tamas is more predominant than in the others. The upward ascent consists in the gradual increase of the sattva element and diminution of the tamas, since pain is a particular modification of the quality of rajas. Strictly speaking, the guṇas mingle, combine and strive in every fibre of our being. Their relative strength determines our mental character. We have men of elevated spirituality, passionate force and depressing apathy. Tamas, if predominant, brings in inertia, ignorance, weakness, incapacity, want of faith and disinclination to act. It produces the coarse, dull, ignorant type of human nature. The individuals in whom the rajas is predominant are intrepid, restless and active. Sattva develops the critical, balanced, thoughtful nature. While the three guṇas are present in different proportions in all men, the seer, the saint and the sage have sattva highly developed in them; the warrior, the statesman and the forceful man of action have rajas highly developed in them. Again, though the guṇas affect every part of our natural being, relatively speaking, the three guṇas have their strongest hold in the three different members of it, namely, mind, life and body. The Sāṁkhya recognises no merit in sacrifices. It does not exclude the sudras from higher studies. The teacher is not necessarily a Brahmin, but he who has freed himself. The winning of a good teacher depends on our previous conduct.

INDIAN PHILOSOPHY, II, pp. 310–11

Yogi Discipline

The ancient thinkers of India had a good working knowledge of what may be called the science of metaphysics, and were quite familiar with cryptesthesia and other kindred powers. They tell us that we can acquire the power of seeing and knowing without the help of the outer senses, and can become independent of the activity which we exercise through the physical senses and the brain. They assume that there is a wider world about us than we are normally able to apprehend. When some day our eyes open to it, we may have an extension of our perception as stupendous as a blind man has when he first acquires sight. There are laws governing the acquisition of this larger vision and manifestation of latent powers. By following the principles of the Yoga, such as heightening the power of concentration, arresting the vagaries of mind by fixing one's attention on the deepest sources of strength, one can master one's soul even as an athlete masters his body. The Yoga helps us to reach a higher level of consciousness, through a transformation of the psychic organism, which enables it to get beyond the limits set to ordinary human experience. We discern in the Yoga those cardinal conceptions of Hindu thought, such as the supremacy of the psychic over the physical, the exaltation of silence and solitude, meditation and ecstasy, and the indifference to outer conditions, which make the traditional Hindu attitude to life appear so strange and fantastic to the modern mind. It is, however, conceded, by many who are acquainted with it, that it is a necessary corrective to our present mentality, overburdened with external things and estranged from the true life of spirit by humdrum toil, material greed and sensual excitement.

INDIAN PHILOSOPHY, II, pp. 336–7

The goal of jīva is detachment and independence. It is not compatible with the human relationships of family life, society, etc., and accordingly the Yoga is said to be an unethical system. Ethical considerations cannot have any place in a system that aims at the breaking of all bonds connecting the individual to the world. The criticism is one which we have frequently met. The ethical pathway alone helps us to reach the goal of perfection, though the latter takes us to a region beyond good and evil. Salvation is the realisation of the true nature of the self which is obscured by so many impurities. We can get rid of them only by effort and discipline. The Yoga is much more emphatic than many other systems in holding that philosophy cannot save us. What we stand in need of is not subtleties of disquisition but control of will. We must subdue the inner turmoil of emotion and passion. The true philosopher is a physician of the soul, one who helps us to save ourselves from the bondage of desire.

INDIAN PHILOSOPHY, II, p. 364

Saṁkara

Śaṁkara appeared, at one and the same time, as an eager champion of the orthodox faith and a spiritual reformer. He tried to bring back the age from the brilliant luxury of the Puranas to the mystic truth of the Upaniṣads. The power of the faith to lead the soul to the higher life became for him the test of its strength. He felt impelled to attempt the spiritual direction of his age by formulating a philosophy and religion which could satisfy the ethical and spiritual needs of the people better than the systems of Buddhism, Mīmāṁsā and Bhakti. The theists were veiling the truth in a mist of sentiment. With their genius for mystical experience, they were indifferent to the practical concerns of life. The Mīmāṁsaka emphasis on karma developed ritualism devoid of spirit. Virtue can face the dark perils of life and survive only if it be the fine flower of thought. The Advaita philosophy alone, in the opinion of Śaṁkara, could do justice to the truth of the conflicting creeds, and so he wrote all his works with the one purpose of helping the individual to a realisation of the identity of his soul with Brahman, which is the means of liberation from saṁsāra. In his wanderings from his birthplace in Malabar to the Himālayas in the north he came across many phases of worship, and accepted all those which had in them the power to elevate man and refine his life. He did not preach a single exclusive method of salvation, but composed hymns of unmistakable grandeur addressed to the different gods of popular Hinduism—Viṣṇu, Śiva, Śakti, Sūrya. All this affords a striking testimony to the universality of his sympathies and the wealth of natural endowment. While revivifying the popular religion, he also purified it. He put down the grosser manifestations of the Śakta worship in South India, and it is a pity that his influence is not perceptible in the great temple of Kālī in Calcutta. In the Deccan, it is said that he suppressed the unclean worship of Śiva as a dog under the name of Mallāri, and the pernicious practices of Kāpālikas whose god Bhairava desired human victims. He condemned branding or marking the body with hot metallic designs. He learned from the Buddhist Church that discipline, freedom from superstition and ecclesiastical organisations help to preserve the faith clean and strong, and himself established ten religious orders of which four retain their prestige to-day.

The life of Śaṁkara makes a strong impression of contraries. He is a philosopher and a poet, a savant and a saint, a mystic and a religious reformer. Such diverse gifts did he possess that different images present themselves, if we try to recall his personality. One sees him in youth, on fire with intellectual ambition, a stiff and intrepid debater; another regards him as a shrewd political genius, attempting to impress on the people a sense of unity; for a third, he is a calm philosopher engaged in the single effort to expose the contradictions of life and thought with an unmatched incisiveness; for a fourth, he is the mystic who declares that we are all greater than we know. There have been few minds more universal than his.

INDIAN PHILOSOPHY, II, pp. 449–50

The logic of Śaṁkara has in it elements of both agnosticism and mysticism. The absolute is the unattainable goal towards which the finite intellect strives, and when it reaches its consummation thought ceases to be what it is in our empirical life, and passes into a higher and more direct form of apprehension in which it and its object can no longer be distinguished. Logical dialectic helps us to overcome the errors into which thought of necessity falls. The inconsistencies and the incompleteness in which Śaṁkara's theory of knowledge is content to remain are not due to any defects in his reasoning, but are the inevitable imperfections of a philosophy which tries to go to the depth of things. For him knowledge is so vital and error so fatal that he will not admit anything as true unless it stands the scrutiny of logic.

INDIAN PHILOSOPHY, II, p. 526

Inconceivable though it is, the Ātman has nothing to do with the individual's life history, which it so faithfully attends and accompanies. Assumed as the constant witness, the Ātman serves merely as the screen or the basis on which mental facts play. We cannot say that they grow out of it, for the real is not affected by what is confused with it. Things do not alter their nature simply because we do not rightly understand them. How does the unchanging Ātman appear as limited, how can the eternal light of intelligence be darkened by any agency whatever, since it is free from all relations? It is the old question 'How does the real become the phenomenal?' It is the relation of Ātman to the upādhis of body, senses, mind and sense-objects that accounts for its phenomenal character; but this relation between the Ātman and the psychological self is inexplicable, māyā, or mysterious. If Ātman is eternal freedom and pure consciousness, and wants nothing and does nothing, how can it be the source of movement and desire in the embodied self? 'A thing,' it is answered, 'which is itself devoid of motion may nevertheless move other things. The magnet is itself devoid of motion, and yet it moves iron.' When we speak about the relation of the finite selves to the infinite Ātman, we are at the mercy of the finite categories, which do not strictly apply.

INDIAN PHILOSOPHY, II, p. 604

Asceticism is a charge that is frequently levelled against Śaṁkara's ethics. In a hundred ways Śaṁkara urges that there is never anything worthy of pursuit in empirical life. Illness and death come, if not to-day then to-morrow, to ourselves and those whom we love, and nothing remains of all we love on earth but dust and ashes. Nothing on earth can offer a sure foothold for the soul of man. The futility of saṁsāra and attachment to it are indicated in the familiar story of the traveller who, to save himself from the wild beast that is pursuing him, gets into the dried-up well. But at the bottom of the well there is a dragon with its jaws wide open to devour him. He cannot get out for fear of the wild beast, he dare not descend for fear of the dragon, and so he catches hold of a branch of a wild plant growing out of a crevice of the well. He grows tired and feels that he must soon perish. Though death awaits him on either side, he still holds on, clinging fondly to the wild plant, but lo! there are two mice, one black and the other white, gnawing the trunk of the wild plant. It will soon give way and break off and the traveller cannot escape the jaws of death. Even so, we who are travelling on the circuit of saṁsāra know the pitfalls of our life, know that all things to which we cling will inevitably perish, but in spite of it all, we find some drops of honey on the leaves of some wild plant and are busy licking them. Though we know that the dragon of death awaits us, though we know that the white mouse and the black, day and night, are gnawing through the branches to which we cling, we still are tempted by the tree of life. The dragon is there, but that does not matter, the honey is sweet. We take the tree for the truth and do not want to face the terrible fact that nothing in saṁsāra can satisfy the infinite in man. Saṁkara tells us that the supreme fulfilment is the result and reward of supreme renunciation. It is reached when desire is dead and pleasure and pain alike are cast away. The most perfect virtue and the loftiest intellectual vision are inadequate for the purpose of spiritual perfection. Saṁkara insists on a life of self-sacrifice and asks us to free ourselves from attachment to the body. The enemy of the soul is not the body as such, but our bondage to the body and the sense of mineness. The released soul before death is possessed of a body, but its presence is not inconsistent with the freedom of spirit. It is because the body in the ordinary individual offers a thousand hindrances to the free growth of the spirit that we find Śaṁkara arguing that the life of the spirit is repressed and hampered by union with the material body. The appearance of asceticism is due to the repeated exhortations to crucify the flesh with the passions and the lusts thereof.

INDIAN PHILOSOPHY, II, pp. 631–2

Man has to purify himself from the defilements of the world, strip off all clothing, leave behind everything unworthy. He must break away from the slavery of selfhood, passion and sense. A deliberate surrender of all personal feelings and preferences, a self-stripping to the point of apparent nothingness, a 'flight of the alone to the alone,' means eternal life. The emphasis in Śaṁkara is not on retirement from the world, but on renunciation of the self. It is easier to flee from the world than from the self. Śaṁkara asks us to suppress our selfishness, and, if that requires solitude and retirement, these are advised as means to an end. One who has completely shaken himself free from selfishness is at liberty to take upon himself the task of the world. His attitude will be not world-seeking or world-fleeing, but world-saving. The perfect man lives and dies, not for himself, but for mankind. It is, however, true that Śaṁkara asks us to be in the world but not of it, even as a drop of water is on the lotus leaf without getting mixed up with it. The part of wisdom is to dream with our eyes open, to be detached from the world without any hostility to it.

INDIAN PHILOSOPHY, II, pp. 632–3

Rāmānuja

Rāmānuja and Hegel hold that the ultimate reality is a one containing many. For them the rational is the real: God and the world are both real. The indeterminateness of intuition and the mystery of reality do not appeal to them. They are interested not in the real in itself but the real for thought, which has an element of negativity in it. The process of thought consists in the continual absorbing and transcending by mind of its own discrepant and rebellious parts. So all spiritual life is an unceasing struggle with refractory elements. Divine life is regarded as an eternal activity. To think of the world as a logical unity or a single system is to think of it as the manifestation of one perfectly determinate principle in an infinity of details. But we should not overlook the difficulties attending this conception of the highest as the concrete universal or the union of the finite and the infinite.

INDIAN PHILOSOPHY, - II, pp. 559–60

Śaṁkara and Rāmānuja are the two great thinkers of the Vedānta, and the best qualities of each were the defects of the other. Śaṁkara's apparently arid logic made his system unattractive religiously; Rāmānuja's beautiful stories of the other world, which he narrates with the confidence of one who had personally assisted at the origination of the world, carry no conviction. Śaṁkara's devastating dialectic, which traces all—God, man and the world—to one ultimate consciousness, produces not a little curling of the lips in the followers of Rāmānuja. Śaṁkara's followers outdo the master, and bring his doctrine perilously near atheistic mentalism. The followers of Rāmānuja move with as much Olympian assurance through the chambers of the Divine mind as Milton through the halls of heaven. Yet Rāmānuja had the greatness of a religous genius. Ideas flowed in on him from various sources—the Upaniṣads and the Āgamas, the Purānas and the Prabandham—and he responded to them all with some side of his religious nature. All their different elements are held together in the indefinable unity of religious experience. The philosophic spirit was strong in Rāmānuja, so, too, was his religious need. He tried his best to reconcile the demands of the religious feeling with the claims of logical thinking. If he did not succeed in the attempt to give us a systematic and self-contained philosophy of religion, it should not surprise us. Much more remarkable is the deep earnestness and hard logic with which he conceived the problem and laboured to bridge the yawning gulf between the apparently conflicting claims of religion and philosophy. A thin intellect with no depth of soul may be blind to the wonders of God's ways, and may have offered us a seemingly simple solution. Not so Rāmānuja, who gives us the best type of monotheism conceivable, inset with touches of immanentism.

INDIAN PHILOSOPHY, II, pp. 720–1

Theology and Philosophy

A theologian generally takes his stand on a particular denominational basis. As a member of a particular religious community, he sets himself to systematise, expand and defend the doctrines of his school. He accepts his creed as the truth with which his religion stands or falls. The philosopher, on the other hand, in so far as he is a philosopher, does not confine himself to any one religion, but takes religion as such for his province, without assuming that the religion in which he is born or which he accepts is the only true religion. In Śaṁkara we find one of the greatest expounders of the comprehensive and tolerant character of the Hindu religion, which is ever ready to assimilate alien faiths. This attitude of toleration was neither a survival of superstition nor a means of compromise, but an essential part of his practical philosophy. He recognised the limitations of all formulas and refused to compress the Almighty within them. No reasonable man can think that his sect has weighed and measured God and set forth the result of the process in its own infallible creed. Every creed is an adventure of faith, an approach to experience. It is the instrument which leads to the vital religious experience; and if the reality of religious experience acquires a meaning for the individual who sincerely seeks after God in this or that particular form, it is impertinent for us to ask him to change his creed. Śaṁkara was not so fanatical as to question the religious experiences of those who claim to have direct contact with God through their respective tributes of faith and love. If men of radically different convictions are able to secure the same results of moral quickening, peace of mind and rapport with the central spiritual reality, he allowed them to have their own views.

INDIAN PHILOSOPHY, II, p. 652

Philosophy has its roots in man's practical needs. If a system of thought cannot justify fundamental human instincts and interpret the deeper spirit of religion, it cannot meet with general acceptance. The speculations of philosophers, which do not comfort us in our stress and suffering, are mere intellectual diversion and not serious thinking. The Absolute of Śaṁkara, rigid, motionless, and totally lacking in initiative or influence, cannot call forth our worship. Like the Taj Mahal, which is unconscious of the admiration it arouses, the Absolute remains indifferent to the fear and love of its worshippers, and for all those who regard the goal of religion as the goal of philosophy —to know God is to know the real—Śaṁkara's view seems to be a finished example of learned error. They feel that it is as unsatisfactory to natural instincts as to trained intelligence. The world is said to be an appearance and God a bloodless Absolute dark with the excess of light. The obvious fact of experience that, when weak and erring human beings call from the depths, the helping hand of grace is stretched out from the unknown, is ignored. Śaṁkara does not deal justly with the living sense of companionship which the devotees have in their difficult lives. He declares that to save oneself is to lose oneself in the sea of the unknown. Personal values are subordinated to impersonal ones, but the theist protests that truth, beauty and goodness have no reality as self-existent abstractions. An experience that is not owned by a subject is a contradiction in terms. Truth, beauty and perfection speak to us of a primal mind in whose experience they are eternally realised. God himself is the highest reality as well as supreme value. Moreover, the innermost being of God is not solely the realisation of eternal truth or the enjoyment of perfect beauty, but is perfect love which expends itself for others. The value of the finite world to the Spirit of the universe lies in the spirits to whom he has given the capacity to make themselves in his own image. The spirits themselves possess a value in the sight of God, and not merely their degrees of intelligence or virtue, abstractly considered, which they happen to realise. It follows that they are not made simply to be broken up and cast aside.

INDIAN PHILOSOPHY, II, pp. 659–60

CHRISTIANITY

SCRUPULOUS sensitiveness in our search for truth is making it difficult for us to accept doubtful authority or half-heard traditions. If genuine religious belief has become for many a phenomenon of the past, it is because religions confound eternal truth with temporal facts, metaphysics with history. They have become largely a traffic with the past. For example, in Christendom theology is busy with such questions as: Are the Scriptures inspired? How shall we explain the divergencies in the accounts of the life of Christ? How shall we reconcile the Biblical account of creation with modern science? Were the Old Testament prophecies fulfilled? Shall we believe in the New Testament miracles? Acute thinkers spend their time and energies in finding modern ideas in ancient texts or reading meanings into them which are not there. So long as the life of Jesus is regarded as a mere event in history which occurred nineteen hundred years ago there can be no understanding of what that life should mean to us. A study of comparative religion has broken down the barriers behind which dogmatists seek to entrench themselves and show that their own religion is unique. Besides, the anthropomorphic conceptions which look upon God as king or conqueror, father or lawgiver, the good shepherd or the righteous judge possessing to a transcendent degree the qualities of power and virtue which we most admire in human beings, seem to many somewhat archaic and crude. They tend to hide the central truth that God is Spirit and that the only real worship is that which is in spirit and truth.

EASTERN RELIGIONS AND WESTERN THOUGHT, p. 59

For the orthodox Christian, the coming of the Kingdom is catastrophic and not the peaceful outcome of an ever-widening process of evolution, an intervention of God cutting right into history and not springing from it. He despairs of earth and lives in apocalyptic hopes of divine intervention.

EASTERN RELIGIONS AND WESTERN THOUGHT, p. 74

In the light of our present knowledge of man's history and the vastness of the cosmos it seems anomalous, if not absurd, to imagine that the earth or the human species or any historic individuals in it form the centre of things. Our earth is parochial and our citizenship on it a triviality. Geocentrism in cosmology and anthropocentrism in philosophy and Buddhocentrism or Christocentrism in religion are on a par. Man is the centre of all things only in the sense, as Professor Eddington has pointed out, that he stands midway in size between an atom and a star. He is almost exactly as much larger than an atom as a star is larger than a man. To those whose minds are dazed by the new knowledge of science, the orthodox theologians seem to be like men talking in their sleep.

AN IDEALIST VIEW OF LIFE, pp. 27–8

The Hindu philosophy of religion starts from and returns to an experimental basis. Only this basis is as wide as human nature itself. Other religious systems start with this or that particular experimental datum. Christian theology, for example, takes its stand on the immediate certitude of Jesus as one whose absolute authority over conscience is self-certifying and whose ability and willingness to save the soul it is impossible not to trust. Christian theology becomes relevant only for those who share or accept a particular kind of spiritual experience, and these are tempted to dismiss other experiences as illusory and other scriptures as imperfect. Hinduism was not betrayed into this situation on account of its adherence to fact.

THE HINDU VIEW OF LIFE, p. 19

Jesus had an abhorrence of dogma and never encouraged the metaphysical and theological complications which are responsible for a good deal of casuistry, intolerance, and obscurantism. His chief opponents were the high priests and the pharisees, who insisted on salvation by orthodoxy alone. In both the Catholic and the Protestant forms, though in different degrees, Christianity has become a religion of authority, finding its seat in a tradition believed to be supernaturally imparted. Instead of the contemplation of the formless we have the definitisation of the deity in the personal God or His incarnation. Instead of indifference to rites and formulas, we have the greatest insistence on them. Though Jesus paid little attention to organisation, elaborate ecclesiastical structures have emerged from His teaching. In the effort to establish a kingdom not of this world, the most realistic of ecclesiastical organisations has been built up on earth. The teaching of Jesus had for its aim the making of spiritual souls who are above the battle of creeds and of nations, but it is used to make loyal members of the Church.

EASTERN RELIGIONS AND WESTERN THOUGHT, p. 272

PREDESTINATION

AGAIN, the theory of election is fraught with great danger to ethical life. The predestinarian scheme of thought puts an excessive strain on the other parts of Madhva's theology. The moral character of God is much compromised and the qualities of divine justice and divine love are emptied of all meaning and value. Individual effort loses its point, since whether one believes oneself to be the elect or the non-elect, one is bound to lapse into indifferentism and apathy. If we do not know what we are destined for, we may work on to purify ourselves. In the absence of knowledge we may at least have hope. But this theory will overwhelm us in despair and raise the question: Is not God playing a practical joke on us when he implants in us a desire for heaven while making us unfit for it? Unless we are in a position to believe in the spiritual possibilities of every one who bears the human form divine, we cannot have a really useful ethics. In certain passages Mahdva says that the individual soul is of the form of knowledge and bliss, though it is not conscious of this nature, while God is eternally conscious that he is of the nature of knowledge and bliss. The distinction, therefore, between God and man, however great, is not one of kind. The essence of each soul may perhaps represent its degree of obscuration, but it is difficult to prove that there are eternal essences persisting in souls even when they are released. In all this we are simply transferring the distinctions of experience to the kingdom of God.

INDIAN PHILOSOPHY, II, pp. 750–1

THE PRESENT SITUATION

It was long held that the mechanical view, while adequate in the realm of matter, fails us when we come to organic life. The delicate adjustments of the bodily organs to the functions they serve, the eye for seeing and the ear for hearing, seem to require a different explanation. But the carefully selected illustrations of design, contrivance and adaptation used by Paley and Butler to prove the reality of God conceived as a gigantic craftsman, are now shown to be the working of the principle of adaptation to environment. Nature in her blind thirst for life has filled the earth with innumerable types. The offspring of living organisms are never exactly alike. They vary slightly both from the parents and from one another. Variations which help the individuals to live more easily tend to survive. Those individuals which do not share these variations pass out. By a continuous piling up of small variations spread over a long period of time, Darwin held, a new species is produced. Though this view has suffered modifications in detail—variations are said to be discontinuous and far from gradual or by minute stages—the general theory is not much disturbed. The story of continuous development through the whole of animate nature suggests the working of an automatic mechanism. No principle outside the natural world is needed to account for it. In a closed world governed by uniform laws, no spiritual principle can interfere. The elaborate pictures given in our ancient scriptures of the defeat of God's original intention by a host of fallen angels or the attribution of the countless woes of ages to the erroneous choice of an imaginary chief which involved the whole of posterity in ruin and corruption do not have any semblance of truth for those familiar with the larger concepts of development through countless centuries. We cannot be sure that species move on to higher stages of development in orderly sequence. Ever so many degenerate and some die out altogether. No sooner has some form of existence perfected itself than it proceeds to decay. The progress we have achieved is the result of the terrible method of trial and error. Struggle and suffering, disease and death are such pregnant facts that if there is any ruling power in the universe, it may be fate or chance or careless gods, but in no case a beneficent providence. Man is nothing more than the latest of a long series of living creatures, and he did not arrive on this planet faultless and finished but is being slowly ground into shape by the shocks of circumstance. The half-men of the Paleolithic age, the Neanderthal and the Piltdown bones show how near the apes primitive men were. Anthropomorphism loses its point when the rise of humanity is seen to be a curious accident and its career a mere episode in cosmic history. The history of humanity measured against the inconceivably long vista of time is but the twinkling of an eye. Human beings confined to an infinitesimal part of space seem so far removed from the main plan of the universe. We cannot be certain that man is the last and the supreme utterance of life. The chain may well extend to other links which may be as different from him as he is different from the amoeba. Man is a relatively recent arrival on earth. He has possessed and governed it for less than a thousandth part of its existence. Gigantic reptiles and dinosaurs ruled it for millions of years and might have thought that they would continue for ever. Man to-day regards himself as the final triumph of biological evolution and has come to stay! Man may be another unsuccessful experiment which the Unknowable, not quite certain of its direction, is making. Even if the evolution of life on earth does not proceed higher than the human species, science threatens us with a possibility of its extinction. The solar system, we are told, is like a clock which is running down and its processes are irreversible. Though it may not stop in our own day, its eventual doom can hardly be averted. Scientific evidence seems to suggest that the universe which has crawled by slow stages into its present shape is making for a condition of universal death.

The values for which we struggle are only a flash in the pan and will disappear sooner or later. The cosmic process is but a weaving and unweaving of forms in which the values we cherish find precarious and brief embodiment. Ethical principles are but general rules for the guidance of human conduct and owe their significance to the developing society in which they arise. Our sense of duty is at bottom the 'herd instinct' which is found even among animals. In obedience to this instinct the interests of the individual are subordinated to those of the group. The authority of conscience is of purely social origin and does not require any reference to a supernatural power. There is not a single human act which society has not at one time approved and at another condemned. Though standards change, life seems to be meaningless without them and so the myth of morality is invented. And science tells us how the illusion is born. Morality is a working arrangement and its sanction is social necessity. As morality is a matter of convention, society has a right to alter or amend it, if it judges such modifications in the line of its interests. There is no God commanding us into a prescribed mode of behaviour.

Ethical rules are objective only in the sense that they are independent of this or that individual and not in the sense that they are unconditional commands or that they assume that 'good' is an unanalysable and ultimate quality.

AN IDEALIST VIEW OF LIFE, pp. 24–7

The present unrest, it is clear, is caused as much by the moral ineffectiveness of religion, its failure to promote the best life, as by the insistent pressure of new knowledge on traditional beliefs. There are a few intellectual snobs with whom it is a sign of accomplishment to ridicule religion. To care for religion is to be old-fashioned; to be critical of it is to be in the movement. A reading democracy which is necessarily imperfectly educated feels it its duty to reject traditional control when it does not understand the reasons for its claims. Scepticism does not cost us much. It is faith that requires courage nowadays. Besides these denying spirits we have the much larger number who have outgrown the faith but are unwilling to break away for fear of the pharisees. Our concern, however, is with those who find themselves while willing, yet incapable of belief. Their souls have grown more sensitive and so their difficulties are deeper and their questions more insistent. Their doubt is an expression of piety, their protest a kind of loyalty. In the depths of the human soul lies something which we rationalise as the search for truth, a demand for justice, a passion for righteousness. This striving for truth and justice is an essential part of our life. We do not need an Aristotle to tell us that the pursuit of knowledge is our highest duty and the only permissible excesses are the excesses of the intellect. The disorders due to the disturbance of our minds are preferable to the bondage of the human spirit. This is not the first time in the history of the world that the age was felt to be transitional and religion held to be untenable. It is said—though I cannot vouch for its authenticity—that the first words uttered by Adam and Eve as they stepped out of the gate in the garden of Eden were, 'We live in times of transition.' Every period is one of transition. Through discord and confusion lies progress. It happens in the sub-human level; it is willed in the human. The spirit of man can change the direction of the march. The invention of what is needful at a particular moment, of the device which will help us to adapt ourselves to the new situation, has the same significance as the development at the right time of the new variation which alone is adapted to the altered conditions. At a time when humanity is struggling to rise from a state of subjection to authority to one in which perfect self-determination is possible, we need the assistance of creative minds. The prophet souls and not the priest minds, the original men of understanding and not the mechanical imitators of the inherited habits, are needed to help our wandering generation to fashion a goal for itself. Prophecy is insight. It is vision. It is anticipating experience. It is seeing the present so fully as to foresee the future.

AN IDEALIST VIEW OF LIFE, pp. 49–51

The character of a civilisation is derived from its conception of the nature of man and his destiny. Is man to be regarded in biological terms as the most cunning of animals? Is he an economic being controlled by the laws of supply and demand and class conflicts? Is he a political animal, with a raw excessive politicalism occupying the centre of the human mind, displacing all knowledge, religion and wisdom? Or has he a spiritual element requiring him to subordinate the temporal and the expedient to the eternal and the true? Are human beings to be understood in terms of biology, politics or economics, or are we to take into account their family and social life, love of tradition and place, love of religious hopes and consolations whose history goes back far beyond the oldest civilisations? The deeper meaning of the war is to help us to realise the imperfect conception of man's nature and his true good, in which we are all involved in our way of thinking and our way of living. If we are not kind to one another, if all our attempts to bring peace on earth have failed, it is because there are obstacles, malicious, selfish and wicked, in the heart and mind of man which our way of life does not check. Our achievement in perfecting life's material apparatus has produced a mood of self-confidence and pride, which has led us to exploit matter instead of informing and humanising it. Our social life has given us means but denied us ends. A terrible blindness has afflicted the men of our generation, who do not hesitate to gamble in human sorrow, through hard economic laws in times of peace, and aggression and cruelty in times of war. The exclusion of the element of spirit from the human is the primary cause of the supremacy of matter which we find so burdensome and oppressive. The defeat of the human by the material is the central weakness of our civilisation.

RELIGION AND SOCIETY, pp. 21–2

Those who tell us that asceticism is superfluous, that contemplation is perilous, and the precept 'be perfect' means 'make a success of life and attend if possible to the perishing moment,' do not understand the high destiny of man. A reborn living faith in spiritual values is the deepest need of our lives. Only religion which demands as its first principle individual change, the substitution of the divine for the dark image in the soul, can create that new heart in the peoples, can give them the courage and the faith to be consistent and change their life and institutions which are so barbarous, in a thousand details which loyalty to their religion demands.

EASTERN RELIGIONS AND WESTERN THOUGHT, p. 114

The West is passing through a new Renaissance due to the sudden entry into its consciousness of a whole new world of ideas, shapes, and fancies. Even as its consciousness was enlarged in the period of the Renaissance by the revelation of the classical culture of Greece and Rome, there is a sudden growth of the spirit to-day effected by the new inheritance of Asia with which India is linked up. For the first time in the history of mankind, the consciousness of the unity of the world has dawned on us. Whether we like it or not, East and West have come together and can no more part. The spatial nearness is preparing the way for a spiritual approximation and interchange of treasures of mind and imagination. If we are nurtured exclusively on the past of Europe or of Asia we cannot consider ourselves to be cultivated. The thought and experience of one-half of humanity cannot be neglected without peril. If we are to correct the narrowness resulting from a one-sided and exclusive preoccupation with either Eastern or Western thought, if we are to fortify our inner life with the dignity of a more perfect and universal experience, an understanding of each other's cultures is essential. It is a foolish pride that impels some of us to combat all external influences. Every spiritual or scientific advance which any branch of the human family achieves is achieved not for itself alone, but for all mankind. Besides, there is no power possessed by any race of men that is not possessed in some measure by all. The difference is one of degree. The mysticism of ancient India or the rationalism of modern Europe is only a fuller development of something which belongs to man as man. To the observer of the essential drifts of the dawning world, it is clear that we are in an age when cultures are in fusion. To penetrate to the heart of a civilization we ought to study its secret springs of thought, its religious ideals. Religion has been from the beginning the bearer of human culture. It is the supreme achievement of man's profound experience. It is the deepest kind of life reflecting the different phases, complex and conflicting, of human living. Millions of minds, their thoughts and dreams, go to make a religion. A large part of the world received its religious education from India. In spite of continuous struggle with superstition and theological baggage, India has held fast for centuries to the ideals of spirit.

EASTERN RELIGIONS AND WESTERN THOUGHT, pp. 115–16

The more general tendency is to reduce religion to the level of our practice, to argue that the pattern of our civilisation is, if not completely religious, at least on the way to it. Even though we have costly and magnificent churches and gorgeous ritual and music, we are not quite so brazen as to say that our commerce and athletics, our selfish nationalism and international anarchy are religious. Among both individuals and nations we admire the rich and the successful, and the strong and the powerful. Anyone who has not at least five hundred a year is a figure to be sneered at, and any weak nation which believes in selflessness in others is to be pitied, for it deserves to be wiped out, off the map. If any people are unwilling to convert their corporate manhood into a military arm, they are decadent. To succeed in life, we must believe in life and its values, which are economic success and political power. By a multitide of sophisms we persuade ourselves that God expects us to believe in them and will help us if we pursue them with vigour and enterprise and deceit and cunning, if necessary. Whatever we do, we do in the name of God.

EASTERN RELIGIONS AND WESTERN THOUGHT, p. 289

We require a religion which is both scientific and humanistic. Religion, science, and humanism were sisters in ancient India; they were allies in Greece. They must combine to-day if we are to attract all those who are equally indifferent to organised religion and atheism, to supernaturalism and nihilism. We need a spiritual home, where we can live without surrendering the rights of reason or the needs of humanity. Reverence for truth is a moral value. It is dearer than Buddha or Jesus. Truth is opposed, not to reason or the Greek spirit, but to dogma and fossilised tradition. We cannot rest the case of religion any more on dogmatic supernaturalism.

EASTERN RELIGIONS AND WESTERN THOUGHT, p. 294

Our vision is dimmed and our way lost. We have taken a wrong twist which has dispossessed, impoverished and embittered our agricultural population, corrupted, coarsened and blinded our workers, and given us millions of children with blank faces, dead eyes and drooping mouths. Beneath our present bafflement and exasperation the bulk of the people retain a hunger for the realisation of the old dream of genuine liberty, real self-respect; of a life where none is rich and none is poor, where the extremes of luxury and leisure are abolished and where industry and commerce exist in a simple form.

MAHATMA GANDHI, pp. 24–5

We are inclined to give too much importance to exceptional incidents by seeing them in distorted perspective.

What we do not sufficiently realise is that these setbacks, blind alleys and disasters are only a part to be viewed in relation to the background of the general tendency at work over the centuries. If we could only get a detached view of the continued effort of mankind, we would be amazed and profoundly moved. Serfs are becoming free men, heretics are no longer burned, nobles are surrendering their privileges, slaves are being freed from a life of shame, rich men are apologising for their wealth, militant empires are proclaiming the necessity of peace, and even dreams of the union of mankind are cherished. Yes, we have even to-day the lust of the powerful, the malice of knaves, the lies of the hypocrites and the rise of arrogant racialism and nationalism; yet one would be blind if one did not see the great tradition of democracy which is universal in its sweep. Unceasing is the toil of those who are labouring to build a world where the poorest have a right to sufficient food, to light, air and sunshine in their homes, to hope, dignity and beauty in their lives.

MAHATMA GANDHI, p. 20

RELIGIOUS SITUATION

WHAT are the sources of this growing unrest in religion? The unscientific character of religious beliefs and the unsocial nature of religious practices are responsible for the increasing indifference to religion. Without any deliberate propaganda or missionary effort, the spirit of criticism and secular culture have been spreading throughout the world, as an accompaniment of the new industrial civilisation. A scientific frame of mind has become a part of the mental equipment of even ordinary men and women. We are therefore intellectually unable to profess faith in beliefs associated with religion. While science speaks to us of interstellar spaces and astronomical immensities religion asks us to believe in the creation of the world in 4004 B.C. When the pre-Copernican theory of the universe prevailed, the long story of development from the nebulae to man as the consummation of a purposive evolutionary process was not unreasonable. Now the earth has ceased to be the centre of creation and man on earth cannot be regarded as the crown of the evolutionary process. In the known universe the milky way is a tiny fragment. In this fragment the solar system is a mere speck, our earth is an infinitesimal dot. On this dot mankind is crawling about desperately struggling to effectuate its own extinction. Even if it escapes this fate, the history of man is but a brief episode in the life of the solar system which is itself doomed to destruction. While myths of creation are repudiated by the sciences of astronomy and geology conceptions of mind and soul are revolutionised by biology and psychology. Historical events on which religions are based are explained in a different way by anthropology and history. Supernatural phenomena are given natural explanations. Secular education leads men to think that there is no rational or moral meaning of the universe, that all is mechanical and amoral, that values have no validity apart from accidents of time and place, that things dictate to man the law of his intrinsic development, that the individual *per se* does not count, that men are accountable only to themselves, that spiritual life is wishful thinking, and when this earthly journey is ended, it is all over with man. We sweep the skies with the telescope and find no trace of God, we search the brain with the microscope and find no sign of mind. However much religion may have served humanity in the infancy of the human race, in an age of reason like our own, it is said that there is no longer any need for it.

HIBBERT JOURNAL, vol. 44, 1945–6, pp. 296–7

Authoritarian religions cannot help us. Even as modern man, when overcome by a sense of fear and insecurity, resorts to the principles of force, authority and suppression of freedom in the political sphere, so also in the religious sphere when he gets tired of himself and is disillusioned about life, he tends to throw himself on a superhuman transcendental power or social collectivity. When he cannot bear to be his own individual self, and longs to feel security by getting rid of his burden, he takes shelter in a person or an institution. The frightened individual who clings to something outside of him gains security no doubt, but it is at the expense of his integrity as an individual. He is saved from making decisions or assuming responsibility. His doubts are resolved by his relationship to the power to which he has attached himself. But he is disturbed and dissatisfied at the root for the emergence of his individual self cannot be reversed. The great spirits like the Buddha, Socrates and Jesus set the freedom of the human spirit above the world. Above all social loyalties is loyalty to another order of reality. The loneliness of great men who in crises exasperate even their friends, who stand for the supernatural, for the human, for the world as against a race or a nation or a class, moves us all. To win all the power on earth at the cost of the freedom of the soul is the third temptation. Jesus did not succumb to it but died on the Roman cross for the truth he would not surrender.

HIBBERT JOURNAL, vol. 44, 1945–6, pp. 300–1

The Greek inheritance has enabled the West to remake the world. Earth, sea and air have been made to yield to the service of man. Though the triumphs of intellect are great, its failures are not less great. Some of the finest things of life have escaped its meshes, which the uncouth and unlettered peasants, who lived more naturally and professed animistic conceptions of life, had possessed. Pitiful and sordid as had been their estate, they had a hope in their hearts, a spark of poetry in their lives and a feeling of exaltation in their human relationships. Ignorant and superstitious they might have been, but wholly forsaken they were not. Their lives were not empty and devoid of content. They had their deep affections, a sense of the great value of the little things of life, love, companionship and family attachments, an element of mystery in their make-up, a faith in the unseen which was the consolation of their dreams. The business of intellect is to dispel the mystery, put an end to the dreams, strip life of its illusions and reduce the great play of human life to a dull show, comic on occasions but tragic more frequently. The primitive cults which helped their adherents to live healthily and happily on their own plane are dismissed as crude superstitions. Everything is stripped of soul, of inner life. This world is all, and we must rest content with it.

HIBBERT JOURNAL, vol. 35, 1936–7, p. 29

Rodin created that wonderful statue called *The Thinker*, the colossal figure of a man sitting with his head bent, his eyes staring out into space, his brows wrinkled with thought, his face furrowed with suffering and tense with concentration and looking at . . . what? Looking down the ages, age after age, world after world, he finds man advancing along the corridors of time, trying to control his difficult, discordant, divided self and asking, Shall we never escape from this division? Must we go on for ever aiming at the high and doing the low? Is it our fate to be for ever split selves, with bewildered outlooks, aspiring after ideals of universal human decency and practising policies which lead us to universal barbarism? Why, why cannot we have the courage and the selflessness, the vision and the generosity to regulate our affairs on principles of equity and justice? Life is a supreme good and offers the possibility of happiness to everyone. No generation has ever had so much opportunity. Yet the blessings of the earth have turned into curses on account of the maladies which afflict us, envy and hatred, pride and lust, stupidity and selfishness. Man, as he exists to-day, is not capable of survival. He must change or perish. Man, as he is, is not the last word of creation. If he does not, if he cannot adapt himself and his institutions to the new world, he will yield his place to a species more sensitive and less gross in its nature. If man cannot do the work demanded of him, another creature who can will arise.

HIBBERT JOURNAL, vol. 35, 1936–7, p. 33

The end of each individual is to reveal in his life the timeless element, to incarnate the Divine idea, to establish its supremacy in the instrumentality of nature. The end of man is to recognise that the Divine is his real self, to discover and consciously realise it. There is no one who is entirely lost. Even as there is not absolute non-existence, so also there is not absolute evil. If man misses his destiny in this life, the destiny to advance from time to eternity, he will fulfil it in another. Nature is not in a hurry. The human individual who lives in time has to realise his possibilities, resolve contradictions, conquer the world and transform it instead of destroying and abandoning it to its fate. He must become a symbol of human integrity and attain a constant and unique form in the midst of incessant flux. He must battle with ignorance and imperfection and take possession of the infinite kingdom.

When the individual rises to wisdom, he does not escape from life. To be rid of the ego is not to be rid of life. Negatively we may say that he is released from hampering egoism; positively he has realised his spiritual destiny and has become united with the spirit of the universe. He knows that the same universal self dwells in all beings. A single impulsion runs beneath all the adventures and aspirations of man. Those realised souls who have a perception of the secret solidarity of the whole creation cut across all artificial ways of living and work for the wider, all-embracing vision. As the freed individual belongs to both orders of time and eternity, he leads a new kind of life, centred in truth and devoted to the practice of love. He works on earth with his spirit in heaven.

HIBBERT JOURNAL, vol. 44, 1945–6, p. 304

WAR

MAN, unless he is sadistic, is happy when he is gentle and merciful. There is joy in creation and misery in destruction. The common soldiers have no hatred for their enemies, but the ruling classes by appealing to their fear, self-interest and pride seduce them from their humanity. People in whom rage and hatred are factitiously produced fight one another because they are simple men trained to obedience. Even then they cannot put rancour in their killing. It is discipline that compels them to do what they hate. The ultimate responsibility lies with the Governments that are implacable and pitiless. They have imprisoned simple people and diminished their humanity. Men who delight in creation are drilled to form armies, navies and air fleets that are meant for destruction. We applaud murder and make mercy a thing of shame. We forbid the teaching of truth and command the spreading of lies. We rob both our own people and strangers of decency, of happiness and of life, and make ourselves responsible for mass murders and spiritual death

MAHATMA GANDHI, p. 37

It is a delusion to think that the nations are becoming too well educated and enlightened for wars. It is the sand in which we are burying our heads. It was observed in the last war that there was a better feeling among the masses of people than among the intellectuals. All this is because our thought is superficial. We do not think, because we are afraid that it may cost us dearly. It may upset our plans and schemes. We simply do what the other man does. The pull of the crowd is irresistible. In the Middle Ages the Church exercised a tyranny over the people; now the jingoes do it. A few demagogues and adventurers with their control over the press and the radio lay down the law, and the masses unthinkingly march to their death. Our wills, our minds are not our own. A machine stronger than ourselves has made tools of us all. We are dressed in uniforms which enter our flesh. The silence of steel suppresses our sense of values. We are unable to look facts in the face. Hatred is made so agreeable and dished up so attractively that we revel in it, though we have no knowledge of the thing we hate. We are called cowards if we do not hate enough to kill. What is called discipline substitutes the certainty of being killed if we do not go to the front for the chance of being killed if we go. We take the risk and gain credit for courage. We wish for the death of brothers in arms, and slay without hatred, like machines, men whom we do not know, against whom we have absolutely no cause of emnity. Held in the terrible vice of wartime discipline, which forbids one to think, we kill by command, not by conviction. We are brave enough to suffer, to accept sorrow, but not brave enough to reject suffering for the sake of superstition. We fight for our symbols, trade, property, empire, symbols which have become stale and petrified. We have not the courage to cast off the old symbols, the outworn traditions, which have become fetters. We cannot shake them off, because the process of false education starts in the nurseries. Tradition and romance and all the unconscious influences of education have been for centuries directed towards the glorification of the independent sovereign State and the suppression of others as the most direct expression of loyalty to one's own State.

EAST AND WEST IN RELIGION, pp. 87–9

The Hindu scriptures commend non-violence as the supreme duty; but they indicate occasions on which departure from this principle is permissible. We live in a society governed by certain laws, codes and customs which are not ideal, but have made compromises, which use armies, police and prisons. Even in such a society, we can live a life inspired by love to all men. While keeping the ideal before us and always striving towards it, the Hindu view recognises the relative justification of laws and institutions, because of the hardness of men's hearts. 'The wise know that both dharma and adharma are mixed with injury to others.' But these institutions are stepping-stones to a better order. While we need not lose ourselves in the pursuit of an impossible perfection, we must strive perpetually to eliminate imperfection and grow towards the ideal. Progress in civilisation is to be judged by the number and character of the occasions on which exceptions to the rule are permitted. Brutal methods of teaching the young, crude punishments of offenders, are to be abolished. The ideal of ahiṁsā must be cherished by us as a precious goal, and deviations from it are to be accepted with regret. A somewhat similar view is to be found in the teaching of Jesus and his followers.

RELIGION AND SOCIETY, p. 206

Our whole conception of the state requires alteration. Power and force are not the ultimate realities in human society. A state is a group or association of persons inhabiting a certain defined territory, with a common government. When a certain state is said to be more powerful than another, all that is meant is that its inhabitants, on account of certain advantages, numbers, strategical position, control of raw materials, or development of agriculture and industry, or arms, are in a position to compel inhabitants of other areas by force to do what they wish them to do. In early days, the physically stronger individual exercised control over the weaker, even as powerful states control weaker ones. Is this in principle different from the husband who beats his wife, from a dacoit who holds up someone at a street corner and robs him of his purse, or an employer who breaks a strike? This faith in force is a disease that has twisted and tortured the world. It deprives us of our manhood. A world in which the unspeakable fiendishness of war is possible is not worth saving. We must get rid of the social order, the nightmare world which is maintained by loud-speakers, floodlighting and recurrent wars. War sets up a vicious circle, a dictated peace with revenge, resentment and thirst for revenge on the part of the vanquished, and war again. Humility becomes us all. A new technique, a revolutionary one, has to be adopted. About the feud between the houses of Capulet and Montague, Mercutio, slain in the duel, in the insight of the dying moment, cries: 'A plague o' both your houses.' That bitter feud of one house against the other was cut across by a love that broke the vicious circle of its hate. In that final moment of the play Capulet says: 'O brother Montague, give me thy hand.'

RELIGION AND SOCIETY, pp. 221–2

AUTHORITARIANISM

(1) *Politics*

SOCIAL groups are formed in the interests of survival. They have no other purpose than furthering their own material good, by force and fraud, if necessary. Economic welfare is the end of all existence. The principles of evolution offer a scientific basis for militaristic imperialism. When powerful groups exploit the weaker races of the earth, they are but instruments for furthering the evolution of higher biological forms which has brought us from amoeba to man and will now complete the journey from Neanderthal man to the scientific barbarians of the modern world. The great powers constitute themselves into God's policemen for preserving law and order in all parts of the globe, into missionaries for civilising the weaker races, who are treated as creatures of a lower order, annoying intruders with a different mental cast and moral constitution. The Jews are not the only people who called themselves the Chosen Race. Others also have faith in their mission, though this faith is based not on revelation but on historic or legendary destiny. To fulfil their destinies nations are converted into military machines and human beings are made into tools. The leaders are not content with governing men's bodies, they must subjugate their minds. They must transmit faith in their messianic mission to the community at large. Without much effort they gain the goodwill of the decadent and the discontented, the poor and the unemployed, the adventurous and the opportunist and the young and the eager who have neither ideal nor guiding star but only erring minds and quivering hearts. The seeds of rampant nationalism find fertile soil in the unpledged allegiance of emancipated minds. An abnormal state of moral and mental tension results where free thinking is replaced by dull obedience, moral development by moral quietism, feeling of humanity by arrogance and self-righteousness.

CONTEMPORARY INDIAN PHILOSOPHY, pp. 262–3

The human individual is emptied of his own history, of his destiny, of his inward past. He is regarded as an aimless, drifting, credulous creature who, without a mind and will of his own, is driven like cattle, or moulded like wax, by those who have elected themselves to be his rulers. If liberty is freedom to be our real selves, this anxiety to rid us of liberty shows the fall of man. This surrender of the human soul to the swarm makes us into a race of animals gifted with reason. For, in the animal world, the individual is less important than the race.

Natural rights, liberty of conscience, are proclaimed to be 'liberal illusions' behind which the capitalist order lies entrenched. The dialectical process relates to the social substance of humanity. No individual can be good unless the social structure to which he belongs is good. To the religious thesis that we cannot change society unless we change men, the Marxian opposes the view that we cannot change men unless we change society.

We live in a world dominated by machines and natural science. Mechanical views of human nature are more acceptable. Psychoanalysis looks upon human beings as helpless slaves of their subconscious impulses, capable of being refashioned by medical men. Behaviourism looks upon the mind of the human infant as a perfectly blank sheet, on which we can inscribe anything we please. Human wickedness is traced to bad glands and unwise conditioning. The Marxist believes that the soul is wholly a product of circumstances, especially the social and the economic. Its acts of thinking, valuing and deciding are not the expression of its free and spontaneous activity, but are the psychological by-products of the social environment to which it is exposed. Marx wrote: 'It is not the consciousness of men that determines their existence, but on the contrary their social existence determines their consciousness.' His successors reduce this view to a rigid determinism, and hold that consciousness is a mere epiphenomenon. When the circumstances change of themselves through the inexorable laws of history, individuals will change also. Social factors determine human behaviour. Spinoza had observed that if a stone falling through the air could think, it might well imagine that it had freely chosen its own path, being unaware of the external causes. Even so, ignorance of the natural causes of our behaviour leads us to think that we are different from the falling stone. But everything occurs as the result of the unalterable process of nature. Man is an object in nature, whose likes and dislikes are determined by conditions as rigid as those which govern the fall of bodies, the growth of plants or the rotation of planets. The ideologies of opposing schools are only rationalisations, or attempts to find specious reasons for actions which are really the resultants of economic interests. A mechanistic view which makes human actions blind and automatic is the result.

RELIGION AND SOCIETY, pp. 56–7

(2) *Religion*

Confronted by such a cold view, those who are anxious for religion are building for themselves different ways of escape. We have first of all the fundamentalists—and they are not confined to America or to Christianity—who ask us to shut our eyes to the facts of modern thought and inquiry. They want us to go by the beaten track, like horses in blinkers, looking neither to the right nor to the left. They call upon us to repeat blindly the sayings of the illustrious dead. It does not matter whether they are illustrious or not, as Aldous Huxley says, what matters is that they should be dead. For the fundamentalists, education is the greatest calamity. There is much to be said for ignorance; but as education has come to stay, fundamentalism does not seem to have any future. A few intellectuals, who are apparently weary of the perpetual flux of the modern time-spirit and are therefore anxious to come to an anchor somewhere, also seek refuge in fundamentalism.

THE RELIGION WE NEED, p. 8

A few openly repudiate any divine or spiritual reality in the world. They assert that there is no purpose in the world and any day anything might happen. The world is changing in unknown directions and not even God knows what will come next. Let us not be fooled into falsehood by blind faith or imaginative piety. A considerable number of this school assert selfishness in morals and anarchism in social life. The more heroic among the atheists ask us to make the best of this world with all its cruelties and imperfections. For them the highest religion is endurance and enterprise, the strength of soul to suffer and strive.

It is no use repudiating the religious implications of science. I believe that the growing dissatisfaction with established religion is the prelude to the rise of a truer, more spiritual, and so more universal religion. The scientific temper is opposed to the acceptance of dogma. The scientist pursues truth without any bias or presuppositions. He does not start with the idea that his conclusions should square with dogmas. Religion as revelation or dogma has no appeal to the believer in science. If religion starts with the assumption of an absolute God and tries to infer his characteristics, the nature of the world, etc., from its initial assumption, it tends to become mere scholasticism or deductive development of dogma. If there is an omnipotent and beneficent God, then the world which is his creation must be good. Evil is only an appearance. The suffering of the wicked is God's judgment and the suffering of the righteous is God's test. Science has no sympathy with such *a priori* schemes of revealed religion. It starts not so much with the creator as with the creation. It studies the facts of nature and society and frames an idea of God to suit them. It approaches the problems of religion in an attitude of empiricism or experimentalism.

THE RELIGION WE NEED, pp. 10–11

Where religion has not been herself the oppressor upholding darkness by violence, she lends her authority to the oppressors and sanctifies their pretences. That religion is worth little, if the conscience of its followers is not disturbed when war clouds are hanging over us all and industrial conflicts are threatening social peace. Religion has weakened man's social conscience and moral sensitivity by separating the things of God from those of Caesar. The socially oppressed are seduced by hopes of final adjustment in a celestial fatherland, a sort of post-mortem brotherhood. No wonder religion is condemned as a piece of capitalistic propaganda. The workers and wage-earners have come to discover themselves and are demanding an opportunity for a fuller and deeper life. Anxious as they are for a new social order based on justice and creative love, they stand out of religious organisations which preach contentment and *status quo*. The social revolutionaries contend that religion blocks the way to all progress. It is a bourgeois prejudice and superstition which must be rooted out at any cost. Spiritually an external or ceremonial religion is good for nothing; materially it has failed to stop the strong man from exploiting his weaker brother; psychologically it has developed traits which are anti-social and anti-scientific. As for its aesthetic and metaphysical satisfactions, they can easily be fostered by the spread of science and art, morality and social service and a living faith in human brotherhood. Communism is the new religion; Lenin is its prophet and science its holy symbol.

AN IDEALIST VIEW OF LIFE, pp. 46–7

While the economic and political forces are bringing people closer together, religions are doing their utmost to maintain the inner barriers that divide and antagonise peoples. To the Hindus the Buddhists are heretics, even as the early Christians were atheists to the polytheistic Romans. Catholics would sooner see one an atheist than an Anglican. Religion engenders a great love for a great hate. Every religion has its popes and crusades, idolatry and heresy-hunting. The cards and the game are the same, only the names are different. Men are attacked for affirming what men are attacked for denying. Religious piety seems to destroy all moral sanity and sensitive humanism. It is out to destroy other religions, not for the sake of social betterment or world peace, but because such an act is acceptable to one's own jealous god. The more fervent the worship the greater seems to be the tyranny of names. By a fatal logic, the jealous god is supposed to ordain the destruction of those who worship him under other names. The view that God has entrusted his exclusive revelation to any one prophet, Buddha, Christ, or

Mohammad, expecting all others to borrow from him or else to suffer spiritual destitution, is by no means old-fashioned. Nothing is so hostile to religion as other religions. We have developed a kind of patriotism about religion, with a code and a flag, and a hostile attitude towards other men's codes and creeds. The free spirits who have the courage to repudiate the doctrine of chosen races and special prophets and plead for a free exercise of thought about God are treated as outcasts. No wonder that even the sober are sometimes tempted to think that the only way to get rid of religious fear, conceit and hatred is to do away with all religion. The world would be a much more religious place if all the religions were removed from it.

IDEALIST VIEW OF LIFE, pp. 44–5

Even if life be aimless, man must pursue some dream. To deny him hope is to take away his interest in life. Religions exploit this need, this fundamental insufficiency of an all-pervading positivism, this primitive hunger for fellowship. The fugitive character of life makes man fondly hope that his life is not at an end with the death of the body, that it cannot be true that the suffering of the innocent meets with no reward and the triumph of the wicked with no requital. It must be that man does count. Religions attempt to satisfy this fundamental need of man by giving him a faith and a way of life, a creed and a community, and thus restore the broken relationship between him and the spiritual world above and the human world around. While the prophet founders of religions declare that the community is world-wide and make no distinctions between the Jew and the Gentile, the Greek and the barbarian, the traders in religion declare that the greatness of one's own creed and group is the end and coercion and violence are the ways to it.

They develop group loyalties at the expense of world loyalty. Such a bellicose condition is the only one in which life becomes worth while for a large number of people. There is not much to choose between these religions, which exalt belief, bigotry, and preservation of group loyalties and vested interests, and the older, cruder, primitive cults. The later, which are the more sophisticated, are the more dangerous, for they are constructions of intellect interfering with the natural relations of man.

EASTERN RELIGIONS AND WESTERN THOUGHT, p. 39

The spiritual genius who can think out a religion for himself is one in a million. The large majority are anxious to find a shrine safe and warm where they can kneel and be comforted. For them it is a question of either accepting some authority or going without religion altogether. It is catholicism or complete disillusion. The leaders enlarge on the beauty and richness of the worship, the antiquity and order of the tradition, the opportunity for influence and service which the historic Church offers. If we are not to languish as spiritual nomads, we require a shelter, and the Church which is majestically one in creed, ritual, discipline and language, a corporation in which racial and national barriers are obliterated, a kingdom without frontiers, attracts the large majority.

AN IDEALIST VIEW OF LIFE, p. 78

Men not inferior in intellect, not depraved in their morals, not alien to the civilised in their judgments and the values they attach to common things, men like Gandhi and Tagore, plead guilty to being Hindus. Such a faith cannot provoke our disgust or arouse our contempt. It kindles our curiosity. We want to understand the sources of its strength, the springs of its vitality. To shut our eyes to it is an ostrich-like policy which leads nowhere. No wonder that here and there we come across thoughtful missionaries, none too common, however, who tell us that the future of religion consists in a free fellowship of faiths, where by contact and exchange each faith will acquire a new spirit and a new life. The keynote of the new attitude is expressed by the word 'sharing.' The different religious men of the East and the West are to share their visions and insights, hopes and fears, plans and purposes. Unhappily, just as in the political region, so here also this is more an aspiration than an actuality. Comparative Religion helps us to further this ideal of free sharing among religions which no longer stand in uncontaminated isolation. They are regarded as different experiments influencing one another in producing a free and creative civilisation. They are all engaged in the common effort to build a higher and more stable life. They are fellow-workers toward the same goal. It is our duty to shake hands with their followers to-day and attack the forces of selfishness and stupidity, injustice and irreligion.

EAST AND WEST IN RELIGION, pp. 26–7

INTUITION AND INTELLECT

BROODING is thinking with one's whole mind and one's whole body. It is integral thinking. It is making one's whole organism, sense and sensibility, mind and understanding, thrill with the idea. There is no function or organ of the body which is beyond the influence of the mind or the soul. Man is one psyche, one whole, of which body, mind and spirit are aspects. Donne's magnificent lines about the blushing girl describe this oneness:

Her pure and eloquent blood
Spoke in her cheeks, and so distinctly wrought
That one might almost say her body thought.

It is no use mistaking man for a merely intellectual being. His intellect is not his whole being. We must allow the idea framed by reason to sink into the subsoil of man's life and leaven the whole of his nature, conscious and unconscious. The word, the thought, must become flesh. Only such an alteration of the whole psychology of man, such a transformation of his whole being, such integral understanding, is creative in character. Creation is man's lonely attempt to know his own strange and secret soul and its real vocation.

EAST AND WEST IN RELIGION, pp. 81–2

Our anxieties are bound up with our intellectuality, whose emergence at the human level causes a fissure or cleavage in our life. The break in the normal and natural order of things in human life is directly traceable to man's intellectuality, the way in which he knows himself and distinguishes himself from others. *Firstly*, he thinks and imagines an uncertain future which rouses his hopes and fears. The rest of nature goes on in absolute tranquillity. But man becomes aware of the inevitability of death. This knowledge of death produces the fear of death. He worries himself about ways and means by which he can overcome death and gain life eternal. His cry is, Who shall save me from the body of this death? Though he is born of the cosmic process he feels himself at enmity with it. Nature, which is his parent, is imagined to be a threat to his existence. An overmastering fear thwarts his life, distorts his vision, and strangles his impulse. *Secondly*, man's naïve at-oneness with the living universe, his essential innocence or sense of fellow-feeling, is lost. He does not submit willingly to a rational organisation of society. He puts his individual preferences above social welfare. He looks upon himself as something lonely, final, and absolute, and every other man as his potential enemy. He becomes an acquisitive soul, adopting a defensive attitude against society. *Thirdly*, the knowledge of death and the knowledge of isolation breed inner division. Man falls into fragmentariness. He becomes a divided, riven being, tormented by doubt, fear, and suffering. His identity splits, his nucleus collapses, his naïveté perishes. He is no more a free soul. He seeks for support outside to escape from the freezing fear and isolation. He clings to nature, to his neighbours, or to anything. Frightened of life, he huddles together with others. The present nervousness of mankind, where fear is the pervasive element of consciousness, where we are always taking precautions, avoiding entanglements, where life is always on the defensive, where man has lost his community with nature and man, is another name for spiritual death. The world in which we live to-day, the world of incessant fear (*bhaya*) and violence (*hiṁsā*), of wars and rumours of wars, where we are afraid of everything, suspect mines under our feet, snipers in thickets, poison in the air we breathe and the very food we eat, is nothing but the ordinary life of ignorance hurried up, intensified, and exaggerated. The tragedy is that we are not conscious of our ignorance. The more sick, the less sensible.

EASTERN RELIGIONS AND WESTERN THOUGHT, pp. 43–4

While outer knowledge can be easily acquired, inner truth demands an absolute concentration of the mind on its object. So in the third stage of *samādhi* or identification, the conscious division and separation of the self from the divine being, the object from the subject, which is the normal condition of unregenerate humanity, is broken down. The individual surrenders to the object and is absorbed by it. He becomes what he beholds. The distinction between subject and object disappears. Tasting nothing, comprehending nothing in particular, holding itself in emptiness, the soul finds itself as having all. A lightning flash, a sudden flame of incandescence, throws a momentary but eternal gleam on life in time. A strange quietness enters the soul; a great peace invades its being. The vision, the spark, the supreme moment of unification or conscious realisation, sets the whole being ablaze with perfect purpose. The supreme awareness, the intimately felt presence, brings with it a rapture beyond joy, a knowledge beyond reason, a sensation more intense than that of life itself, infinite in peace and harmony. When it occurs our rigidity breaks, we flow again, and are aware, as at no other time, of a continuity in ourselves and know more than the little section of it that is our life in this world.

EASTERN RELIGIONS AND WESTERN THOUGHT, p. 50

But intuition, though it includes the testimony of will and feeling, is never fully attained without strenuous intellectual effort. It cannot dispense with the discipline of reason and the technique of proof. Religion itself may take three forms, primitive or sensuous, reflective, and mystical. Religion in the mystic sense is not a mere speculation of reason or a feeling of dependence or a mode of behaviour. It is something which our entire self is, feels, and does; it is the concurrent activity of thought, feeling, and will. It satisfies the logical demand for abiding certainty, the aesthetic longing for repose, and the ethical desire for perfection. In the great mystics, the *ṛṣis* of the Upaniṣads, Buddha, Śaṁkara, and hundreds of others, holiness and learning, purity of soul, and penetration of understanding are fused in an harmonious whole.

EASTERN RELIGIONS AND WESTERN THOUGHT, p. 63

The normal limits of the human vision are not the limits of the universe. There are other worlds than that which our senses reveal to us, other senses than those which we share with the lower animals, other forces than those of material nature. If we have faith in the soul, then the supernatural is also a part of the natural. Most of us go through life with eyes half shut and with dull minds and heavy hearts, and even the few who have had those rare moments of vision and awakening fall back quickly into somnolence. It is good to know that the ancient thinkers required us to realise the possibilities of the soul in solitude and silence and transform the flashing and fading moments of vision into a steady light which could illumine the long years of life.

INDIAN PHILOSOPHY, II, p. 373

THE RELIGION OF SPIRIT

FOR in the historical evolution of the world first comes inert matter, then life; and so, whether Bergson calls matter the relaxation of spirit or the negative effect thereof, matter presupposes spirit. Only, in matter spirit has not come to itself. Reality is one, though we can describe it as a struggle of two tendencies. It is not a mechanical mixture of two elements but a conflict of two tendencies. It is a current which we call upward when the creative spiritual tendency is conquering and downward when the non-creative tendency is conquering. Becoming, which is the union of the two principles of being and non-being, is alone real. As Hegel would put it, being or life has an impulse to complete itself, and so relates itself to non-being or matter, and passes with it into the higher category of becoming. While becoming is the sole reality, conceptual thought discovers in it being and absolute nought, which is its other. Reality is change, activity, or becoming. The history of evolution is the continuous becoming of being by overcoming its other. The succession of living forms is just the attempt of being to overcome non-being. All the objects of the universe are mixtures of these two tendencies. The relative grades of the objects are determined by the more or less of the creative or the spiritual tendency. The hierarchy of values is determined by the more or less of the spiritual nature. The universe from its beginnings in crude matter to its heights in human persons is struggling towards the attainment of the whole. The life tendency moves on, creating endless forms which advance in the direction of, and beyond, man. When man gives up his subordination to matter, then spirit comes back to its own. But in the universe this goal is never reached.

REIGN OF RELIGION IN CONTEMPORARY PHILOSOPHY, pp. 167–8

Spiritual life expresses itself in art, philosophy and religion, beauty, knowledge and perfection. None of these exhausts the fullness of it.

Knowledge is not a mere acknowledgment of the ideal, but a vision of the spiritual life which is a precious possession of the soul coming out in life on every side. Mere knowledge is vain without love. Immanent idealism does not stop with the consideration that the goal of man is reached when he recognises the presence of the Absolute in him. It is clear that knowing is not being, and he does not truly know who is not stirred to his very depths by the consciousness of the infinite in him.

REIGN OF RELIGION IN CONTEMPORARY PHILOSOPHY, pp. 303–5

According to the Vedānta philosophy it is not correct to speak of a sudden revelation of spirit when we come to life, for even matter is spirit, though in its lowest mode of manifestation. When matter reaches a certain climax of development then life breaks out. Life is a later development or stage of the Real. The Real gradually progresses from one stage to another. We cannot say that the later stage of life is a mere product of the earlier stage of matter. Life is not an extension of matter. It is something different in kind from matter. The evolution of the world is not a mere development, but is a development of the whole or the Real. Both matter and life fall within an all-developing spirit whose very nature is to push onward from one to another and thus reach the full realisation through the very impulse of its own movement. The Vedantic view does not involve the sundering of matter from life. It rejects both mechanism and vitalism. We cannot make life mechanical. The world of mechanism is not the same as the world of life. The two are distinct, but the discontinuity between matter and life is not so great as to justify vitalism. The world of mechanism is the medium in which alone life has its being. Though life is not mechanism, still life dwells in it. To make life mechanical or mechanism alive is to dissolve the differences in an abstract identity. It would be to sacrifice wealth of content and speciality of service for the sake of symmetry and simplicity. To make mechanism alive would be to deprive matter of its specific function in the universe. Dead mechanism has its own purpose to fulfil, its contribution to make to the wondrous whole. It is, therefore, not right to reduce unity to identity. We must recognise the difference between the two as much as their unity. The world of matter exists for the purpose of responding to the needs of life.

REIGN OF RELIGION IN CONTEMPORARY PHILOSOPHY, pp. 416–17

Religion begins for us with an awareness that our life is not of ourselves alone. There is another, greater life enfolding and sustaining us. Religion as man's search for this greater self will not accept any creeds as final or any laws as perfect. It will be evolutionary, moving ever onward. The witness to this spiritual view is borne, not only by the great religious teachers and leaders of mankind, but by the ordinary man in the street, in whose inmost being the well of the spirit is set deep. In our normal experience events happen which imply the existence of a spiritual world. The fact of prayer or meditation, the impulse to seek and appeal to a power beyond our normal self, the moving sense of revelation which the sudden impact of beauty brings, the way in which decisive contacts with certain individuals bring meaning and coherence into our scattered lives, suggest that we are essentially spiritual. To know oneself is to know all we can know and all we need to know. A spiritual as distinct from a dogmatic view of life remains unaffected by the advance of science and criticism of history. Religion generally refers to something external, a system of sanctions and consolations, while spirituality points to the need for knowing and living in the highest self and raising life in all its parts. Spirituality is the core of religion and its inward essence, and mysticism emphasises this side of religion.

EASTERN RELIGIONS AND WESTERN THOUGHT, p. 61

Only when a man rises to dispassion and acts without selfish attachment is he really free. The ego is the knot of our continued state of ignorance, and so long as we live in the ego we do not share in the delight of the universal spirit. In order to know the truth we must cease to identify ourselves with the separate ego shut up in the walls of body, life, and mind. We must renounce the narrow horizon, the selfish interest, the unreal objective. This is an ethical process. Truth can never be perceived except by those who are in love with goodness. Again, the delivery from the illusion is not achieved by means of abstract knowledge. Intellectual progress helps us to clear the mental atmosphere of chimeras and phantoms, of errors and illusions. When these hindrances are removed, the truth of spirit is revealed, self-supported and indubitable, filling our entire horizon. An inward change alone fits souls for eternal life. Besides, our apprehension of reality is by no means final, until it is total. It must embrace the whole of our nature, thought, feeling, and will. Wherever the apprehension is only partial, in thought or feeling or will, there will be discontent and unrest in the midst of repose.

The individual strives to make God-control entire by throwing off all that is impure and selfish. All this means effort. Wisdom is not cheaply won. It is achieved through hard sacrifice and discipline, through the endurance of conflict and pain. It is the perfection of human living, the ceaseless straining of the human soul to pierce through the crushing body, the distracting intellect, the selfish will, and to apprehend the unsheathed spirit. It is intent living, the most fruitful act of man by which he tries to reach reality behind the restless stream of nature and his own feelings and desires. The destiny of the human soul is to realise its oneness with the supreme.

EASTERN RELIGIONS AND WESTERN THOUGHT, pp. 95–6

For the Hindu, the spiritual is the basic element of human nature. Spiritual realisation is not a miraculous solution of life's problems but a slow deposit of life's fullness, a fruit which grows on the tree of life when it is mature. The soul, in the state of ecstasy, enters the stream of life, is borne along in the flowing current of it, and finds its reality in the larger enveloping life. This life of spirit, where freedom from the sense of bodily or even mental limitations and emergence into space of unlimited and infinite life are felt, is not the same as magical mysticism.

EASTERN RELIGIONS AND WESTERN THOUGHT, p. 77

We need not adopt the official attitude of the Churches to the mystic developments. They may fight furiously about the dogmas of the divinity schools, but the common notions of spiritual religion remain, the plain easy truths, the pure morals, the inward worship, and the world loyalty. This spiritual religion is based on a firm belief in absolute and eternal values as the most real things in the universe, a confidence that these values are knowable by man by a wholehearted consecration of the intellect, will, and affections to the great quest, a complete indifference to the current valuations of tribes, races, and nations, and a devotion to the ideal of a world community. These are of the very stuff of truth, however hostile they may seem to the orthodoxies. They are the common possession of the great religions, though they are often embedded in superstitious accretions and irrelevances. The universality of the great facts of religious experience, their close resemblance under diverse conditions of race and time, attest to the persistent unity of the main spirit. The adherents of this creed are the citizens of the world yet unborn, which is still in the womb of time. They belong to a movement that is world-wide; their temple is not the chapel of a sect but a vast pantheon; the believers in this movement are not eccentric or isolated ones, but are scattered throughout space, though united in their struggles and ideals, and their numbers would increase if vested interests were removed and if there were no penalties for religious convictions. Mysticism is there latent in the depths of the world's subconsciousness. It is what all sincere people dream of but what earth hath not yet known. It is coming and is well below the horizon.

EASTERN RELIGIONS AND WESTERN THOUGHT, pp. 296–7

We can pass from time to eternity, from appearance to reality; otherwise philosophy and religion are an irrelevance and there is no point in such passages as 'Be ye holy even as I am holy' or 'Be ye perfect.' If faith lives by the call to which it responds, the responding itself is human. The capacity to recognise the self-disclosure of the divine is in us. We can understand the Word; we can hear the summons from eternity, and that is due to our participation in the divine spirit. If the world and the soul are the creations of God, will not the Creator's presence be evident in them? Time is the moving image of eternity, and experience is the appearance of the Absolute. If we dig a ditch between the two, there can be no passage from the one to the other.

EASTERN RELIGIONS AND WESTERN THOUGHT, p. 302

The world is passing through a period of uncertainty, of worldless longing. It wants to get out of its present mood of spiritual chaos, moral aimlessness and intellectual vagrancy. Burdened and tired to death by his loneliness, man is ready to lean on any kind of authority, if it only saves him from hopeless isolation and the wild search for peace. The perils of spiritual questioning are taking us to the opposite extreme of revivals and fundamentalism in religion. These are only half-way houses to a radical reconstruction of the mind. The uncertainty between dogmatic faith and blatant unbelief is due to the non-existence of a philosophic tradition or habit of mind. The mental suffering of the thinking, when the great inheritance of mankind is concealed by the first views of science, the suffering which is due to the conflict between the old and the new values, which are both accepted, though without reconciliation, is the sign that no upheaval, no crude passion can put out the light of spirit in man. However dense the surrounding darkness may be, the light will shine though that darkness may not comprehend it. Only when the life of spirit transfigures and irradiates the life of man from within will it be possible for him to renew the face of the earth. The need of the world to-day is for a religion of the spirit, which will give a purpose to life, which will not demand any evasion or ambiguity, which will reconcile the ideal and the real, the poetry and the prose of life, which will speak to the profound realities of our nature and satisfy the whole of our being, our critical intelligence and our active desire.

CONTEMPORARY INDIAN PHILOSOPHY, pp. 265–6

All the things of the world are there to be enjoyed by man, but in a spirit of detachment. 'Enjoy by renunciation,' says the Upaniṣad. What matters is not the possession or the non-possession of things but our attitude towards them. The question relates to the desires and the appetites, not to the things to which they are directed. It is what a man is, not what he has, his frame of mind that matters. The *Bṛhadāranyaka Upaniṣad* asks us to use the resources of the world for the unfolding of the spirit. All things are dear, not for their own sake but for the sake of the spirit. To be detached is never to want anything for oneself. If we cannot be satisfied with the beauty of the flower until we pluck it and put it in our buttonhole, we cannot be at peace. From detachment comes wisdom, harmony with the environment, peace. The higher vision is possible only for those who have organised their natures. *Jñāna* or wisdom is a function of being. The path to it is as hard 'as the sharp edge of a razor.'

EASTERN RELIGIONS AND WESTERN THOUGHT, p. 131

The code of ethics adopted by mysticism is noble and austere. It insists that suffering and renunciation are the life-blood of religion. In the splendid phrase of Wilamowitz we must give our blood to the ghosts of our ideals that they may drink and live. The world-accepting suggestions of religions can be easily incorporated in our codes, but the stark element of world renunciation is supremely difficult and we are only too ready to make any shifts and adopt any expedients to eliminate it.

EASTERN RELIGIONS AND WESTERN THOUGHT, p. 295

The four ends of life point to the different sides of human nature, the instinctive and the emotional, the economic, the intellectual and the ethical, and the spiritual. There is implanted in man's fundamental being a spiritual capacity. He becomes completely human only when his sensibility to spirit is awakened. So long as man's life is limited to science and art, technical invention, and social programmes, he is incomplete and not truly human. If we are insolent and base, unfair and unkind to one another, unhappy in personal relationships, and lacking in mutual understanding, it is because we remain too much on the surface of life and have lost contact with the depths. When the fountains of spirit from which creative life of the individual and society is fed dry up, diseases of every description, intellectual, moral, and social, break out. The everlasting vagrancy of thought, the contemporary muddle of conflicting philosophies, the rival ideologies which cut through national frontiers and geographical divisions, are a sign of spiritual homelessness. The unrest is in a sense sacred, for it is the confession of the failure of a self-sufficient humanism with no outlook beyond the world. We cannot find peace on earth through economic planning or political arrangement. Only the pure in heart by fostering the mystical accord of minds can establish justice and love. Man's true and essential greatness is individual. The scriptures could point out the road but each man must travel it for himself.

EASTERN RELIGIONS AND WESTERN THOUGHT, p. 354

We must avoid the cant of the preacher who appeals to us for the deep-sea fishermen on the ground that they are daily risking their lives that we may have fish for our breakfasts and dinners. They are doing nothing of the kind. They go to sea for themselves and the families, not for our breakfasts and dinners. Our convenience happily is a by-product of their labours.

EASTERN RELIGIONS AND WESTERN THOUGHT, p. 371

To be rapt is not to pass beyond one's self but to be intensely one's self, not to lose self-consciousness but to be greatly conscious. Man is not torn out of the ordinary setting of his earthly life. He still has a body and mind, though he knows them to be instruments of his higher life. He does not exult in his own intelligence or seek for his own soul, for he has it no more. If he has gained a transcendent personality and an independence which nothing in this world can touch, it is because not he but the Superspirit lives in him, making him illimitable. While mystic experience has something in common with the delight of the artist or the ecstasy of love, which exceed all law and restriction and indicate the possibility of a real communion with life, it is not a mere glow of feeling. Excited emotionalism, which seeks and strives after sensations and rapturous states of a sensual character, is quite different from perfect insight (*samyag-darsāna*). The contemplative saints assign a subordinate position to images and other sensible presentations. These are symbols which we use to understand, and the symbol is different from experience or understanding. *Jñāna* or *vidyā* is cool, clear-sighted vision. In ecstasy the soul feels itself, or thinks it feels itself, in the presence of God, being irradiated by the light; but we must go beyond it to a stage where the consciousness of being at unity with the divine becomes constant. To have an ecstasy is to look upon the promised land but not to set foot on its soil. It is not beatitude or the perfect spiritual possession of divine reality but is its beginning, the first step here below.

EASTERN RELIGIONS AND WESTERN THOUGHT, p. 78

Ecstasy is not the only way to spiritual life. It is often a perversion of mysticism rather than an illustration of it. As there is a tendency to mistake it for spiritual life, we are warned against it. The spiritual mystics the world over regard ecstasy, visions, auditions as things to be avoided and of secondary importance. They are the anomalies of the life of mystics from which they sometimes suffer, and are the results of an imperfect adaptation to a changed inner world. When the personality of the mystic rises to a level which is disconcerting to his normal self-centred life, certain disorders show themselves. The experience throws an intense strain on the organism. When the seed of the oak is planted in earthen vessels, they break asunder. When new wine is poured in old bottles, they burst. Man must become a new vessel, a new creature, if he is to bear the spiritual light. That is why the Hindu system of Yoga insists on the development of healthy nerves.

EASTERN RELIGIONS AND WESTERN THOUGHT, p. 79

SEX

THE sexual act is not a mere pleasure of the body, a purely carnal act, but is a means by which love is expressed and life perpetuated. It becomes evil if it harms others or if it interferes with a person's spiritual development, but neither of these conditions is inherent in the act itself. The act by which we live, by which love is expressed and the race continued is not an act of shame or sin. But when the masters of spiritual life insist on celibacy, they demand that we should preserve singleness of mind from destruction by bodily desire.

MAHATMA GANDHI, p. 18

RELIGION AS LOVE AND SERVICE

THERE is no other God than Truth, and the only means for the realisation of truth is love or ahiṁsā. Knowledge of truth and the practice of love are impossible without self-purification. Only the pure in heart can see God. To attain to purity of heart, to rise above attachment and repulsion, to be free from passion in thought, word and deed, to be redeemed from fear and vanity, the inconsistencies of our flesh and the discursiveness of our minds must be overcome. Disciplined effort, austere living, tapas is the way to it. Suffering rinses our spirit clean. According to Hindu mythology, the God Siva undertakes Himself to swallow the poison which comes up when the ocean is churned. The God of the Christians gave His Son in order to save mankind. Even if they are myths, why should they have arisen if they did not express some deep-seated intuitions in men? The more you love, the more you suffer. Infinite love is infinite suffering. 'Whosoever would save his life shall lose it.' We are here working for God, called upon to use our life for carrying out His intentions. If we refuse to do so and insist on saving our lives instead of spending them, we negate our true nature and so lose our lives. If we are to be able to follow to the farthest limit we can see, if we are to respond to the most distant call, earthly values, fame, possessions and pleasures of the senses have to be abandoned. To be one with the poor and the outcast is to be his equal in poverty and to cast oneself out. To be free to say or do the right, regardless of praise or blame, to be free to love all and forgive all, non-attachment is essential. Freedom is only for the unconfined who enjoy the whole world without owning a blade of grass in it. In this matter, Gandhi is adhering to the great ideal of the saṅñyāsin who has no fixed abode and is bound to no stable form of living.

MAHATMA GANDHI, pp. 17–18

Only the pure in heart can love God and love man. Suffering love is the miracle of the spirit by which, though the wrongs of others are borne on our shoulders, we feel a sense of comfort deeper and more real than any given by purely selfish pleasures. At such moments we understand that nothing in the world is sweeter than the knowledge that we have been able to give a moment's happiness to another, nothing more precious than the sense that we have shared another's sorrow. Perfect compassion untouched by condescension, washed clean of pride, even of the pride of doing good, is the highest religious quality.

MAHATMA GANDHI, pp. 18–19

'Ahiṁsā or non-violence is the highest duty' is a well-known saying of the *Mahābhārata*. Its practical application in life is satyāgraha or soul-force. It is based on the assumption that 'the world rests on the bedrock of satya or truth. Asatya, meaning untruth, also means non-existence, and satya, or truth, means "that which is." If untruth does not so much as exist, its victory is out of the question. And truth being "that which is" can never be destroyed.' God is the reality. The will to freedom and love is in accordance with reality. When man rejects this will for his own interests, he is rejecting himself. By this act of frustration he is setting himself in opposition to reality, is isolating himself from it. This negation represents man's estrangement from himself, his denial of the truth about himself. It cannot be final or ultimate. It cannot destroy the real will. Reality cannot frustrate itself. 'The gates of hell shall not prevail.' God cannot be beaten. The meek shall inherit the earth and not the mighty who will lose themselves in the effort to save themselves, for they put their trust in unspiritual or unreal things like wealth and death-dealing weapons. Ultimately men are ruled not by those who believe in negation, hatred, violence, but by those who believe in wisdom and love, in inward and outward peace.

MAHATMA GANDHI, pp. 31–2

Love is unity and it comes into clash with evil which is separateness, getting, despising, hating, hurting and killing. Love does not acquiesce in evil, in wrongdoing, injustice and exploitation. It does not evade the issue but fearlessly faces the wrongdoer and resists his wrong with the overpowering force of love and suffering, for it is contrary to human nature to fight with force. Our conflicts are to be settled by the human means of intelligence and good will, of love and service. In this confused world the one saving feature is the great adventure of being human. Creative life assets itself in the midst of death. In spite of all this fear and gloom, humanity is practised by all, by the farmer and the weaver, by the artist and the philosopher, by the monk in the cloister and the scientist in the laboratory, and by all, young and old, when they love and suffer.

MAHATMA GANDHI, p. 32

To be true, to be simple, to be pure and gentle of heart, to remain cheerful and contented in sorrow and danger, to love life and not to fear death, to serve the Spirit and not to be haunted by the spirits of the dead, nothing better has ever been taught or lived since the world first began.

MAHATMA GANDHI, p. 40

The best fruits which we can pluck from the tree of life (saṁsāra) turn to ashes in our mouth. The greatest pleasure palls and even life in heaven (svarga) is evanescent. A mere act of goodness or enjoyment of a sweet melody or contemplative insight may, for the moment, seem to lift us out of the narrowness of our individuality, but it cannot give us permanent satisfaction. The only object that can give us permanent satisfaction is the experience of Brahman (brahmānubhava). It is the supreme state of joy and peace and the perfection of individual development. Unfortunately our trouble arises because we cling to the world, cherish faith in its phantoms and feel disappointed when the mocking semblances of finite satisfactions vanish even as we reach them. 'The individual sinks down in sin and grief so long as he believes that his body is the Ātman, but when he realises that he is one with the self of all things, his grief ceases.' We cannot manipulate reality into accord with any ideal of our mind, but have only to recognise it. Philosophy with Śaṁkara is not the production of what *ought to be*, but is the apprehension of what *is*. A spiritual perception of the infinite as the real leads to peace and joy.

INDIAN PHILOSOPHY, II, pp. 613–14

Right action is what embodies truth, and wrong that which embodies untruth. Whatever leads to a better future existence is good, and what brings about a worse form of existence evil. The individual tries to make good his infinite nature and become more and more godlike. In the empirical world, Īśvara is the highest reality and the world is his creation. The believer in God should love the whole universe, which is a product of God. True peace and excellence lie not in self-assertion, not in individual striving for one's own good, but in offering oneself as a contribution to the true being of the universe. Egoism is the greatest evil, and love and compassion are the greatest good. By identifying ourselves with the social good, we truly gain our real ends. Every individual must subdue his senses, which make for self-assertion; pride must give place to humility, resentment to forgiveness, narrow attachment to family to universal benevolence. It is not so much the deed that is valuable as the will to suppress one's selfish will and assert the will of society. Duties are the opportunities afforded to man to sink his separate self and grow out into the world.

INDIAN PHILOSOPHY, II, p. 614

Moral growth consists in a gradual correction of the individualistic point of view, and when the correction is complete, the moral as such ceases to exist. So long as the latter persists, the ideal is unrealised. The end of morality is to lift oneself up above one's individuality and become one with the impersonal spirit of the universe. But, so long as there is a trace of individuality clinging to the moral subject, this lifting up can only be partial. To attain oneness with the infinite, on the basis of the finite, is evidently an impossible task. To realise the ideal, we must pass beyond the moral life and rise to the spiritual realisation in which the life of finite struggle and endeavour is transcended. So Śaṁkara insists repeatedly on the inadequacy of moral goodness and finite striving, so far as the ideal of perfection is concerned. Karma cannot lead to mokṣa. The finite as finite must be transcended.

INDIAN PHILOSOPHY, II, p. 626

What counts is not outer conduct but inner life. Its torturing problems cannot be solved by a reference to rules. Our secret hearts, our prayers and meditations help us to solve the problems of life. The highest morality therefore consists in developing the right spirit. The secret of moral genius lies in the spiritualising of our consciousness. Moral life is the necessary result of spiritual insight. Till the latter is gained, moral rules are obeyed in an external fashion.

INDIAN PHILOSOPHY, II, p. 629

Bhakti or devotion is a vague term extending from the lowest form of worship to the highest life of realisation. It has had a continuous history in India from the time of the Ṛg-Veda to the present day. Bhakti, in Rāmānuja, is man's reaching out towards a fuller knowledge of God quietly and meditatively. He insists on an elaborate preparation for bhakti, which includes viveka, or discrimination of food; vimoka, or freedom from all else and longing for God; abhyāsa, or continuous thinking of God; kriya, or doing good to others; kalyāṇa, or wishing well to all; satyam, or truthfulness; ārjavam, or integrity; dayā, or compassion; ahiṁsā, or non-violence; dāna, or charity; and anavasāda, or cheerfulness and hope. Thus bhakti is not mere emotionalism, but includes the training of the will as well as the intellect. It is knowledge of God as well as obedience to his will. Bhakti is loving God with all our mind and with all our heart. It finds its culmination in an intuitive realisation of God.

INDIAN PHILOSOPHY, II, pp. 704–5

The Bhakti mārga, or the path of devotion, indicates the law of the right activity of the emotional side of man. Bhakti is emotional attachment distinct from knowledge or action. Through it we offer our emotional possibilities to the divine. Emotion expresses a living relation between individuals, and becomes instinct with the force of religious feeling when it binds God and man. If we do not love and worship, we become shut within the prison of our own egoism. This way, when rightly regulated, leads us to the perception of the Supreme. It is open to all, the weak and the lowly, the illiterate and the ignorant, and is also the easiest. The sacrifice of love is not so difficult as the tuning of the will to the divine purpose or ascetic discipline, or the strenuous effort of thinking. It is quite as efficacious as any other method, and is sometimes said to be greater than others, since it is its own fruition, while others are means to some other end.

INDIAN PHILOSOPHY, I, pp. 558–9

The forms which bhakti takes are contemplation of God's power, wisdom and goodness, constant remembrance of Him with a devout heart, conversing about His qualities with other persons, singing His praises with fellow-men and doing all acts as His service. No fixed rules can be laid down. By these different movements the human soul draws near to the divine. Several symbols and disciplines are devised to train the mind to turn godward. Absolute devotion to God is not possible unless we give up our desires for sense-objects. So yoga is sometimes adopted. The impulse may take any form of adoration, from external worship to a periodical reminder to free us from the preoccupations of life. The Gītā asks us sometimes to think of God, excluding all other objects. This is a negative method. It also requires us to look upon the whole world as a supreme manifestation of God. We have to realise God in nature and self, and so regulate our conduct as to make it expressive of the divine in man. Supreme devotion and complete self-surrender, or bhakti and prapatti, are the different sides of the one fact.

INDIAN PHILOSOPHY, I, p. 563

Vaiṣṇava devotion has used the most intimate human relations as symbols of the relation of man and God. God is viewed as the teacher, the friend, the father, the mother, the child, and even as the beloved. The last is stressed by the Āḷvārs, the *Bhāgavata Purāṇa* and the Bengal school of Vaiṣṇavism. In the best love, as in bhakti, to live in the presence of the beloved is the highest happiness and creative productivity; to live without him or her is pain and despair and barrenness. We think that the use of the symbolism of love is wrong because we assume that sensual attraction is all in all in love; but in true love there is little of sensual attraction. Many women, as well as some men, who in love are above the level of beasts, will protest that love is not a mere search after new sensations. In true love, the two souls trust each other more than all others they have met or known before. The lover is ready to fight the world, endure all privations and feel happy in poverty, exile and persecution, for the sake of the beloved. Even if he or she is sundered from the other through many difficulties, so that reunion seems remote, nay impossible, yet he or she cannot afford to lose the other and, at the risk of losing everything else, keeps alive the eternal link created by mutual love which cannot be broken even by death. The stories of Sīta and Sāvitrī, Damayanti and Śakuntalā have burnt this lesson into the heart of India. No wonder the Indian Vaiṣṇava looks upon God as his beloved, and tries to redirect to God the passions, longings and transports of human love. The bhaktas feel helpless and restless when they lose the presence of God, for nothing else can satisfy them. In many of their hymns we find the cry of the heart for God, the sense of devastating desolation in his absence, the anticipated joy in his fellowship and a sense, real though undefined, of the preciousness of his love. In the rapt utterances of the Vaiṣṇava saints, we feel the ecstatic joy of the mystic desirous of union with God in a spiritual sense. 'Thou splendid light of heaven,' cries Nammāḷvār, 'thou art in my heart melting and consuming my spirit.

When shall I become one with thee?' Deep attachment to God results in an indifference to all else.

The Hindu devotee does not seek to destroy desire, but attempts to lift it from earth to heaven, seeks to withdraw it from creation that he may centre it on the Creator. Maṇavāḷa says: 'The pleasure which arises for the ignorant from sense-objects, the same is called bhakti when directed to God; in the case of Nammāḷvār, this bhakti has become love for the beautiful Lord, hence for Āḷvārs there arises the "love" type of devotion.' While many of those who employ the symbolism of bridegroom and bride are free from all traces of eroticism and morally impeccable, it cannot be denied that there were abuses of it. But such abuses were deviations from the normal path.

INDIAN PHILOSOPHY, II, pp. 707–8

HISTORY OF CIVILISATION

It is a fact of history that civilisations which are based on truly religious forces such as endurance, suffering, passive resistance, understanding, tolerance are long-lived, while those which take their stand exclusively on humanist elements like active reason, power, aggression, progress make for a brilliant display but are short-lived. Compare the relatively long record of China and of India with the eight hundred years or less of the Greeks, the nine hundred years on a most generous estimate of the Romans, and the thousand years of Byzantium. In spite of her great contributions of democracy, individual freedom, intellectual integrity, the Greek civilisation passed away as the Greeks could not combine even among themselves on account of their loyalty to the city-States. Their exalted conceptions were not effective forces, and, except those who were brought under the mystery religions, the Greeks never developed a conception of human society in spite of the very valuable contributions of Plato, Aristotle, and the Stoics. The Roman gifts to civilisation are of outstanding value, but the structure of the Empire of Rome had completely ceased to exist by A.D. 500. Empires have a tendency to deprive us of our soul. Extension in space is not necessarily a growth in spirit. Peace prevailed under the Roman rule, for none was left strong enough to oppose it.

EASTERN RELIGIONS AND WESTERN THOUGHT, p. 254

The Chinese and the Hindu civilisations are not great in the high qualities which have made the youthful nations of the West the dynamic force they have been on the arena of world history, the qualities of ambition and adventure, of nobility and courage, of public spirit and social enthusiasm. We do not find them frequently among those who risk their lives in scientific research, who litter the track to the North or the South Pole, who discover continents, break records, climb mountain heights, and explore unknown regions of the earth's surface. But they have lived long, faced many crises, and preserved their identity. The fact of their age suggests that they seem to have a sound instinct for life, a strange vitality, a staying power which has enabled them to adjust themselves to social, political, and economic changes, which might have meant ruin to less robust civilisations. India, for example, has endured centuries of war and invasion, pestilence, and human misrule. Perhaps one needs a good deal of suffering and sorrow to learn a little understanding and tolerance. On the whole, the Eastern civilisations are interested not so much in improving the actual conditions as in making the best of this imperfect world, in developing the qualities of cheerfulness and contentment, patience and endurance. They are not happy in the prospect of combat. To desire little, to quench the eternal fires, has been their aim.

EASTERN RELIGIONS AND WESTERN THOUGHT, p. 257

THE HUMAN IDEAL

THE *jñāni* or the man of insight has liberated himself from the bondage of fear of life and of death, from the prejudices of his time and place, of his age and country. At one with the universal self, he has the utmost charity and love for all creation. Things of the world do not tempt him, for he is free from the bondage of selfish desires and passions. He does not look upon himself as his own. He has emptied himself of all selfishness. In a famous image, the Upaniṣads declare that the released souls become one with Brahman even as the rivers losing their name and form become one with the ocean.

EASTERN RELIGIONS AND WESTERN THOUGHT, p. 132

The fourfold spirit is present in every member of society and its fruitful development is the test of each one's efficiency. There is no life, in so far as it is human, which is not at the same time an inquiry into truth, a struggle with forces inward and outward, a practical adaptation of the truth to the conditions of life and a service of society. Every one in his own way aims at being a sage, a hero, an artist, and a servant. But the conditions of life demand specialisation within limits. Each one cannot develop within his single life the different types of excellence. As a rule one type of excellence or perfection is attainable only at the expense of another. We cannot erect on the same site a Greek temple and a Gothic cathedral, though each has its own loveliness. The ascetic virtues cannot flourish side by side with the social and the domestic. If you choose to be an anchorite, you cannot be a statesman. A hermit does not know what human love is. A social worker cannot devote his strength to the advancement of knowledge. But wherever we may start, it is open to us to reach the highest perfection.

EASTERN RELIGIONS AND WESTERN THOUGHT, p. 365

Hinduism has given us in the form of the *saññyāsin* its picture of the ideal man. He carries within himself the dynamism of spirit, its flame-like mobility. He has no fixed abode and is bound to no stable form of living. He is released from every form of selfishness: individual, social, and national. He does not make compromises for the sake of power, individual or collective. His behaviour is unpredictable, for he does not act in obedience to the laws of the social group or the State. He is master of his own conduct. He is not subject to rules, for he has realised in himself the life which is the source of all rules and which is not itself subject to rules. The quietude of his soul is strange, for though he is tranquil within, everything about him is restless and dynamic. His element is fire, his mark is movement.

EASTERN RELIGIONS AND WESTERN THOUGHT, p. 381

EPIGRAMS

Our trouble is that society in all countries is in the hands of people who believe in war as an instrument of policy and think of progress in terms of conquest.

MAHATMA GANDHI, p. 36

Thought expires in experience.

INDIAN PHILOSOPHY, II, p. 510

The consideration that the distinction of good and evil is relative to our finite level, does not invalidate its observance in the world of practice.

INDIAN PHILOSOPHY, II, p. 634

We often refuse to admit facts, not because there is evidence against them, but because there is a theory against them.

DHAMMAPADA, p. 24

Every fresh epoch in the progress of thought has been inaugurated by a reform in logic.

INDIAN PHILOSOPHY, II, p. 769

When we think we know, we cease to learn.

HIBBERT JOURNAL, vol. 49, April 1951, p. 221

What is dogma to the ordinary man is experience to the pure in heart.

INDIAN PHILOSOPHY, I, p. 51

The ideas of great thinkers are never obsolete. They animate the progress that seems to kill them.

Preface to INDIAN PHILOSOPHY, I

Truth is a sacred achievement, not a plaything of the dialectician. In the world of spirit none can see who does not kindle a light of his own.

DHAMMAPADA, p. 54

Every seeker after truth is called upon to make a monastic cell in his own heart and retire into it every day.

INDIAN PHILOSOPHY, II, p. 357

The sole spiritual vocation of man consists in the discovery of reality, and not what serves our temporal ends.

INDIAN PHILOSOPHY, II, p. 655

We may climb the mountain by different paths but the view from the summit is identical for all.

THE BHAGAVADGĪTĀ, p. 75

Every civilisation is an experiment in life, an experiment in creation, to be discarded when done with.

EASTERN RELIGIONS AND WESTERN THOUGHT, p. 18

Religion is not so much a revelation to be attained by us in faith as an effort to unveil the deepest layers of man's being and get into enduring contact with them.

IB., p. 21

The unity of all life, which is the intellectual assumption of science, becomes the consuming conviction of the sage.

IB., p. 52

We cannot say that definiteness in conception makes for depth in religion.

IB., p. 59

If we believe absurdities, we shall commit atrocities.

IB., p. 80

A religion ceases to be a universal faith if it does not make universal men.

IB., p. 272

The claim of any religion to validity is the fact that only through it have its followers become what they are.

IB., p. 272

All the religions in the world, like all the women in the world, do not compare with the one that is our own.

IB., p. 336

The worst sinner has a future even as the greatest saint has had a past. No one is so good or so bad as he imagines.

HINDU VIEW OF LIFE, p. 71

We need not confound the familiar with the eternal.

RELIGION AND SOCIETY, p. 17

Bibliography of the Writings of Sir S. Radhakrishnan quoted in this Anthology

The Reign of Religion in Contemporary Philosophy (Macmillan): 1920.

Indian Philosophy (Allen and Unwin): vol. I 1923, vol. II 1926.

The Hindu View of Life (Allen and Unwin): 1927.

The Religion We Need (Ernest Benn): 1928.

An Idealist View of Life (Allen and Unwin): 1932.

East and West in Religion (Allen and Unwin): 1933.

Contemporary Indian Philosophy (Allen and Unwin): 1936.*

Eastern Religions and Western Thought (Oxford, Clarendon Press): 1939.

Mahatma Gandhi (Allen and Unwin): 1939.*

Religion and Society (Allen and Unwin): 1942.

The Bhagavadgītā (Allen and Unwin): 1948.

The Dhammapada (Oxford University Press): 1950.

Also various articles in the *Hibbert Journal*, vols. 32, 35 and 49.

* Dr. Radhakrishnan is a contributor to these volumes.

OTHER TITLES ON INDIAN PHILOSOPHY FROM PILGRIMS PUBLISHING

- **Inspirations from Ancient Wisdom (Anthology)** .... *Pilgrims Publishing*
- **Krishnamurti: Two Birds on One Tree** .... *Ravi Ravindra*
- **Perfume of the Desert** .... *Andrew Harvey and Eryk Hanut*
- **The Atman Project** .... *Ken Wilber*
- **Up From Eden** .... *Ken Wilber*
- **Krishnamurti's Insight** .... *Hillary Rodrigues*
- **The Light of Krishnamurti** .... *Gabriele Blackburn*
- **As the River joins the Ocean** .... *G Narayan*
- **Modern Hinduism** .... *W J Wilkins*
- **The Foundations of Hinduism** .... *Jadunath Sinha*
- **Philosophy of Hindu Sadhana** .... *Nalini Kanta Brahma*
- **The Doctrine of Buddha** .... *George Grimm*
- **Buddhism: Its Essence and Development** .... *Edward Conze*

For Catalog and more Information Mail or Fax to:

PILGRIMS BOOK HOUSE

Mail Order, P. O. Box 3872, Kathmandu, Nepal

Tel: 977-1-4700919 Fax: 977-1-4700943

E-mail: mailorder@pilgrims.wlink.com.np